STRATEGIC
THINKING

D1566712

THOMAS G. BANDY

STRATEGIC
THINKING

How to Sustain Effective Ministry

Abingdon Press™
Nashville

STRATEGIC THINKING:
HOW TO SUSTAIN EFFECTIVE MINISTRY

Library of Congress Cataloging-in-Publication Data has been requested.

ISBN: 978-1-5018-4961-9

17 18 19 20 21 22 23 24 25 26—10 9 8 7 6 5 4 3 2 1
MANUFACTURED IN THE UNITED STATES OF AMERICA

Contents

Preface

The need for this book emerged through my experience consulting with churches along the Gulf Coast after Hurricane Katrina. Beyond the physical damage to church property, there was extraordinary damage to leadership and programming. Churches lost as many as 60 percent of their active congregational members. Some died, some relocated, others simply lost heart and faded away, and many faithful professional and lay ministers simply became exhausted.

Yet in the aftermath of the storm the survivors had accomplished miracles rebuilding their lives, reviving worship, and renewing programs. Church mission teams from all over the country helped both churches and neighborhoods do it. A window of opportunity lasted for approximately three more years. During that time, church leaders were incredibly creative in ministry: property renovated, technology updated, programs revised, money raised, worship contemporized, newcomers welcomed, leadership empowered.

After that, the window of opportunity closed for many churches. Creativity stopped. Veteran members and traditional leaders returned. Churches began to return to past customs, retrench previous programs, and try to recapture the good old days. Was it a psychological longing for stability? Or was it an inability to think out of the box? Whatever the reason, only a few years after the explosion of creativity in the face of disaster, when innovation was the name of the game, it became increasingly stressful to implement even the simplest creative idea. We knew how to react to a crisis, but we didn't know how to think strategically about the future.

What happened in New Orleans after 2005 is a good metaphor for church experience in North America over the past thirty years. In North America tempestuous change is precipitated by the hurricane of post-modern living. Churches have lost as much as 60 percent of their active congregational participants; clergy retired, transferred to other jobs, or burned out; the veteran core leadership died, dropped out, or moved in search of an elusive safety.

Initially this storm created a window of opportunity. Everyone was thinking outside of the box. We planted churches, contemporized worship, multiplied small groups, and expanded local and global outreach. Yet today it is increasingly stressful to implement even the simplest creative idea. Established churches everywhere are gathering the family indoors to recapture the good old days, waiting for the neighborhood to return to normal.

It is too easy, and certainly misleading, to blame the current inertia of the church on the preservation of sacred cows or the lack of imagination in church leaders. Of course we hear stories about controllers and institutional self-centeredness, but the truth is that the vast majority of church leaders (ordered and lay) really do want the church to thrive and the community to be blessed. So what really happened?

- First, we knew how to think *reactively*. We knew how to do quick S.W.O.T. analyses. We could see our strengths and weaknesses, and identify our opportunities and threats. We could *react* to any number of emerging situations. What we couldn't do was think ahead to sustain effective ministry. The creative ideas of today soon became the sacred cows of tomorrow. Just look at all the "contemporary" worship services that are still using 1970s praise music.

- Second, we knew how to *plan programs*. We knew how to choose new curricula, tap new sources of funding, recruit (or prop up) committees, and manage time. We could make incremental changes and launch capital campaigns, hire consultants and manage conflict. What we couldn't do was think ahead to keep pace with society. The five year plan became irrelevant after five weeks. Just remember all those retreats, generating all those strategies, collecting dust in all those closets.

Organizational inertia is what happens when leaders don't know how to *think* strategically. They don't know how sustain trust and align to visions, or hold leaders and members accountable for integrity and purpose. They don't reliably and regularly research community, discern divine presence, and assess effectiveness. And they don't have the confidence to set priorities or the courage to take reasonable risks.

An important distinction must be made. This book is not about strategic *planning*. The very word *plan* suggests a blueprint, a step-by-step instruction manual, or some other fixed and repeatable process. Modern people imagined a kind of logical assembly line that promised to reproduce effective churches that were essentially alike if they only followed the instructions. Postmodern people understand that such an assembly line doesn't work now and perhaps never did. Each church is just too unique. The world is moving too fast. There are too many surprises.

The alternative, however, is *not* to throw up your hands in despair, simply react to whatever happens, somehow muddle through, or surrender to some authority (individual or institutional) that will tell you what to do. It is possible for leaders to *think* strategically. There is a method for solving problems and recognizing opportunities. There is a way to make good decisions and timely adjustments to get measurable results.

Strategic *thinking* is about drawing a line from organizational identity—through the changing mission field—to a desired mission result. The tactics are not irrelevant, but they are at best secondary and always delegated to whatever team is doing the work at any given time. Planning today is usually done on the spur of the moment, in response to changing conditions. And if a tactic doesn't work, the last thing you want to do is repeat it.

I usually avoid sports metaphors, but a football analogy seems obvious. The coaches of a football team must think strategically but trust tactically. They combine teamwork and motivation across the gridiron to score a touchdown. The plays they call are on the spur of the moment. And they trust the players to find the ways to get it done. The fullback dances through gaps and avoids tackles any way he wants. The quarterback scans the options and throws the ball anywhere he wants. But they both need to gain yards and achieve touchdowns. There really isn't a plan. Victory depends on the ability of everyone (coaches and players) to *think* strategically and adapt appropriately.

Strategic *thinking* always involves an element of risk. The fullback may fumble, and the quarterback might throw an interception. If the game depended on strategic *planning*, that would be a disaster. But since the game really depends on strategic *thinking*, these setbacks are only frustrating. We may rage or laugh, but in the end we learn and adapt. We keep trying and experimenting until we win.

Strategic thinking requires self-discipline and organizational discipline. It's work. Unfortunately most churches (and many nonprofit and for-profit organizations) don't do it.

One reason is that churches have lost touch with demographic change. I will say more about this later, but for now it is helpful to note that church leaders operate with assumptions about demographic and lifestyle benchmarks and trends that are woefully out of date. For example, church leaders persist on stereotyping people by race, ethnicity, age, and family status. They don't realize that this data is irrelevant in an age of diversity. There are multiple (and multiplying!) lifestyle segments with high proportions of people of the same race, ethnicity, age, or family status that don't behave the same way or share the same ministry expectations. Yet churches still talk in generalizations about "African Americans" and "Hispanics," "youth" and "seniors," and "singles" and "families" as if they did. Rather than think strategically, they merely tweak programs.

This leads to the second reason church leaders avoid strategic thinking. They are overwhelmed. It is not simply that they struggle to keep pace. They are trying not to fall too far behind, but the critical mass of church membership will no longer be able to support their traditions and pensions. They don't have time or energy to do the research, evaluate and prioritize ministries, and manage the stress of change. They are too busy comforting aging members, maintaining aging properties, repeating traditional liturgies, or sustaining programs that were most effective in the 1960s or 1980s.

It becomes a vicious cycle. Church leaders fail to keep up with demographic change; demographic change overwhelms and undermines the effectiveness of their ministries; the pressure builds and they have less time and energy to keep up with change. This vicious cycle has encouraged church leaders to take short cuts. This is why the favored alternative to strategic thinking has become S.W.O.T.

S.W.O.T. is a relatively simple and easy way to survey the "Strengths," "Weaknesses," "Opportunities," and "Threats" facing the congregation at any given point in time. Most of this overview depends on internal surveys of the membership. Some of this depends the priorities of the denomination. A bit of this depends on feedback from social services and other mission partners. And almost none of this depends on actual research among the publics of the neighborhood.

In the end, S.W.O.T. leaves everything to the limited imaginations of the most powerful individuals or factions in the church. They claim "strengths" that are not really there; they identify "weaknesses" that are related only to the fulfillment of membership privileges. The "threats" are challenges to the normative values and biases of individuals and factions inside the church. The "opportunities" are self-serving ways to attract new members to the institution to provide more volunteer and financial support to the institution.

S.W.O.T. keeps strategic thinking inside the box. It is the box defined by the limited risk management of the primary stakeholders inside the institution. Nothing much really changes. The demographic trends within the church grow further and further apart from the demographic trends in the community. The church gets older and remains homogeneous; the community gets younger and more culturally diverse. Meanwhile, lifestyle representation with the membership is increasingly divergent from lifestyle representation in the community. The church becomes an island of self-preservation, and the community largely ignores their existence.

In order go *beyond the box* to be relevant to the changing community, churches must accept more risk. They must be willing to go beyond the comfort zones of members to improve the effectiveness of programs. They must be willing to risk failure and learn from mistakes by implementing

creative new ideas. And they must be willing stop wasting limited resources of time, talent, and money on sacred cows that no longer drive the
church toward its vision.

The challenge, of course, lies in keeping the line between identity and
outcome *straight*. This is not a *curved* line connecting identity, mission,
and results. It is not a wavy line, an intermittent line, or even a partially
angled line. It is not a line that sways one way to protect this self-interest
and another way to protect that membership privilege. It is not a line
that takes a circuitous route to its destination in order to avoid disturbing
some leader's sensibilities or avoid stressing some faction's opinions. It is a
straight line. Nothing else will really do.

Keeping this line *straight* is the art of strategic *thinking*. Some new
ideas will need to be started. Some old programs will need to be ended.
Ongoing tactics will need to be adjusted. Some leaders will need to be
hired or acquired. Some leaders will need to be fired or dismissed. Some
leaders will need to be redeployed. All that effort keeps the line *straight*.
Strategic thinking is not about seeing a need and addressing it. It is
about focusing a purpose and pursuing it doggedly, persistently, and
single-mindedly.

Chapter 1
The Foundation of Strategic Thinking

The church can do nothing without trust. The biblical word for trust is *covenant*. This is the foundation for all decision making in the church. Other sectors of society might call this "corporate culture." Organizations gain a reputation in the community, good or bad, because organizational members habitually behave in certain ways and believe in certain things. That reputation doesn't emerge by accident. It emerges because the organization consciously or unconsciously encourages or discourages its members to function daringly or spontaneously in certain ways. The foundation of trust in a church, however, is more complex than in other organizations. You might say that in a church trust must have both *horizontal* and *vertical* dimensions.

The horizontal dimension is the trust church members have in each other, and that trust expands to include all adherents, visitors, seekers, and strangers who in one way or another, through one church program or another, participate in the work of the church. The horizontal dimension of trust is concretely expressed through consensus regarding core values. Core values guarantee safety. Core values guarantee protection against abuse and manipulation. Core values promise honesty and respect among members and participants that encourage open and nonjudgmental discussion. Core values allow the church to take risks in order to achieve positive outcomes.

1

Core values provide the security that allows the church to fail without fracturing, learn without blaming, and persist without flagging.

The vertical dimension is the trust church members have in God, and that trust expands to give hope to all adherents, visitors, seekers, and strangers. The vertical dimension of trust is concretely expressed through consensus regarding bedrock beliefs. Bedrock beliefs guarantee acceptance and love. Bedrock beliefs reveal the promises of God to protect the church from harassment and manipulation. Bedrock beliefs promise guidance and forgiveness that encourage faithful action. Bedrock beliefs allow the church to take risks in order to pursue great visions. Bedrock beliefs provide security that allows the church to stray without getting lost; grow without elitism; and persist without despair.

The combination of core values and bedrock beliefs becomes the foundation of trust for all strategic thinking. The foundation of trust is not about theory but accountability.

- Core values are embedded in every member, leader, program, and tactic. The public can reasonably expect churches to behave in specific, positive ways. If a member or leader fails (as sinners always do), then the breakdown is called to their attention (usually gently), and the church helps them change. If a program fails (as human efforts always do), then the problem is addressed (usually dialogically), and the church improves the program.

- Bedrock beliefs are confirmed in every member and leader, and reflected in every program and tactic. The public can reasonably expect to hear about hope, see faith in action, and observe spiritual practices among volunteers. Individual members can believe many different things, but in certain things they are united. Programs can develop collaboratively with many mission partners, but the integrity of the church cannot be undermined or ignored.

Before the church can finally do effective strategic thinking, it must define, refine, and celebrate a *foundation of trust*. This is a clear consensus about core values and bedrock beliefs that are the primary vehicles of accountability for every leader and program. Strategic thinkers must be free to imagine, design, implement, and evaluate any tactic no matter how daring or controversial it might be in order to align the church to its vision *without* contradicting or undermining the core values and bedrock beliefs that together form the *foundation of trust* that is the consensus of the church.

For example, church insiders might consider themselves a "friendly church"; but lack of accountability to clear core values has actually given them a reputation as an "elitist church." Or church insiders might articulate specific dogmas and creeds; but they are observed in the hospital or funeral home or in the midst of a crisis as doubtful, cynical, skeptical, or as weak as any unbeliever when it comes to a crunch.

Core Values

Core values are the positive, predictable behavior patterns church members expect of each other in daily routines and daring activities. Core values provide the basis of accountability for how Christians treat people differently than the world does. When a church is behaving at its best, they are respected by neighbors and strangers, community partners and other agencies.

I have written about this many times,[1] teach this over and over again, and still am amazed at how difficult a concept this seems to be for churches to grasp. Our great-grandparents would have more readily understood. Core values are simply the predictable positive behavior patterns that hold a community together. Community is based on predictability. It is shaped around every individual's confidence that they will be consistently treated in certain ways and be held to their commitment to live up to this habitual "social contract" and treat others in the same positive ways.

Perhaps it is the widespread individualization and permissiveness of our culture that makes it so difficult for church people to understand the need for such clear expectations. Yet most people accept these behavioral standards as legitimate in business and nonprofit organizations, and even codify them in human rights legislation. Why is this so difficult for the church? The deeper reason may lie in the trend toward personal religion that is so strong in modern, western culture. We have an exaggerated fear of any kind

---

1. See *Moving Off the Map* (Nashville: Abingdon Press, 1999) and *Spirited Leadership* (Atlanta: Chalice Press, 2007), in addition to numerous magazine articles.

of judgmental attitude based on race, gender, personality, or opinion and an exaggerated pride in our sense of privilege. Accountability is not something church people, in particular, enjoy. They may have to suffer evaluation in other sectors of life, but the church is their ultimate comfort zone.

The trouble, of course, is that the church doesn't exist to guarantee that its members can do whatever they want, behave just like anybody else, and believe anything they wish. It is not an organization dedicated to self-empowerment. It is dedicated to the unique vision that God revealed. It is not intended to be a stress-free oasis or a rock to maintain the status quo. It is God's mission team charged with the biblical goal to bless the world as the spiritual sisters and brothers of Jesus.

The ancient church described positive behavioral expectations as "fruits of the Spirit." Paul went further to refer to core values as *action verbs* rather than *passive nouns*. Every Protestant denomination identified specific standards of behavior for both leaders and members, and although they all recognized the inevitability of sin and the necessity of grace, they also expected Christians to quest for perfection by living a "Godly lifestyle." The details may vary from tradition to tradition, and these are important nuances that distinguish one church from another across the street.

Compare the following list of ancient Christian core values to the current system of accountability in your congregation.

Fruits of the Spirit Galatians 5:22	Apostolic Church Romans 12:1-21	Common Denominational Virtues	Our Website	Our Church
Love	Love genuinely like a brother or sister; Exercise spiritual gifts	Mutual support; Healthy intimacy		
Joy	Rejoice in good times & bad; Glow with the Spirit	Patience and optimism; Inspirational worship		

Peace	Live peaceably with all, without revenge; Overcome evil with good	Peace with justice; Nonviolent protest		
Patience	Be patient in tribulation; Persevere in prayer	Continuing education; Consensus decisions		
Kindness	Associate with the lowly; Weep with those who weep	Pastoral care; Compassionate acceptance		
Gentleness	Live in harmony with others; Be humble, respectful	Teamwork; Care for the most vulnerable		
Generosity	Extend hospitality to strangers; Contribute to the needs of the saints	Radical hospitality; Percentage giving		
Faithfulness	Hold fast to what is good; Transform rather than conform	Sacrificial service; Daily and weekly spiritual practices		
Self-Control	Think with sober judgment; Bless those who harm you	Parliamentary procedure; forgiveness		

Remember that core values are behavioral patterns you model routinely in congregational life and reveal daringly in individual risk. These are behavior patterns you urgently desire to model and therefore teach, train, and use them for individual and congregational confession.

Churches nuance core values in specific ways, for specific contexts. The list of positive behavioral expectations is shared on the home page of a website, posted on the walls of the vestibule, and articulated during worship. One church, for example, translated the core values of the ancient church with this list:

Act with Compassion:	Show concern for all
Hug the World:	Offer friendship and fellowship to all
Exercise the Spirit with Joy:	Engage in regular spiritual practice
Live Up to Our Words:	Maintain integrity between word and deed
Seek Peace:	Demonstrate gentleness and humility
Reach Out:	Serve others with kindness
Live Gently:	Care for all the earth and all creation
Love Others:	Celebrate diversity
Bless and Be Blessed:	Be generous with our time and talent
Turn the Other Cheek:	Seek and give forgiveness

Core values are used as a primary vehicle for accountability in a church, just as they are in any health care, social service, or small business. Visitors feel safer, knowing how they will be treated, and they feel confident that contradictory behavior will be addressed quickly.

Sometimes it is helpful for a church to refine the foundation of trust further by identifying *negative behavior patterns* or *bad habits*. These might also be described as corporate addictions. The church acknowledges that we are all sinners and fall short of expectations at one time or other. Therefore, some churches are equally open about the "temptations" that they struggle to resist. Confession is good for the soul.

A bad habit is a negative, repeated behavior pattern. It is the error or mistake congregational members continually make in spontaneous living and congregational activities. A bad habit is like an addiction. It is a behavior pattern we keep trying to avoid, but keep doing in spite of ourselves. We tend to make excuses and allow this behavior to go unchecked even when it undermines our quality of life together.

The earliest church contrasted the *Fruits of the Spirit* with the *Works of the Flesh*. In time the church defined the Seven Deadly Sins that beset the human condition. And denominations have begun defining particular behavior patterns for which there must be immediate intervention and no tolerance.

Works of the Flesh Galatians 5:19-21	Common Institutional Church Problems	Apostolic Church Seven Deadly Sins
Selfishness	Lack of accountability for shameful behavior among staff, board, & members	Pride
Quarrels	Slander, blackmail, withholding support	
Idolatry	Denigrating people, churches, or religions; elevating my privileges over God's mission	Greed
Dissensions	Turf protection; rivalry for limited resources	
Sexual Misconduct	Tacit acceptance of sexual harassment, flirtation, or disreputable humor	Lust
Licentiousness	Tacit acceptance of spousal or child abuse	
Jealousy	Sacred cows for programs, tactics, or technologies	Envy
Feuds and Factions	Competitiveness for power among staff and lay leaders	
Manipulation	Gossip, failure to preserve confidentiality	Gluttony
Impurity	Conspicuous consumption; obsession with property/ prestige	
Anger	High emotions and cutting remarks	Anger
Enmity	Blind bigotry toward people different from ourselves	
Strife	Factional disputes over ide- ology or worship practices	
(Drunkenness)	Antisocial behavior Do what is convenient, not what is right	Sloth

Core values are further elaborated by the policies of a church for personnel, volunteer training and accountability, and program design.

The value of clarity and consensus around core values is revealed in times of stress. As we shall see, strategic thinking always anticipates stress. I have found it helpful to go *outside* western culture to *aboriginal*

(Australia), *Native American* (USA), or *First Nations* (Canada) cultures to define the set of values that all western lifestyles can embrace as a foundation for conversation or successful mediation. There are numerous tribal examples. I generally focus on ten principles.

1. Listening: Commitment to hear others speak without verbal or physical interruption.

2. Respect: Commitment to respect all people as God's children and honor their right to disagree.

3. Generosity: Readiness to offer extra time, learn new vocabulary, and honor the customs of others.

4. Humor: Openness to laugh at oneself, appreciate irony and paradox, and play with new ideas.

5. Compassion: Commitment to care for the feelings of others, avoid judgement, and heal wounds.

6. Silence: Permission to say nothing, pray at any time, and commune with God in different ways.

7. Symbolism: Sensitivity to body language, facial expressions, and other symbolic ways people communicate what they cannot put into words.

8. Forgiveness: Readiness to endure and overcome hurtful remarks, and reopen opportunities for healing and reconciliation.

9. Wisdom: Commitment to look behind words for deeper meanings, uncover patterns of mutual understanding, and discern how the Spirit is working in unexpected ways.

10. Peace: Commitment to live in tension without anger, bless rather than dismiss another, and search for new reasons to hope.

The principles can be expressed in different ways, with fewer or more words, but these principles mark the boundaries for organizational behavior, especially in times of stress.

Bedrock Beliefs

The second half of the foundation of trust is a clear consensus around what I call "bedrock beliefs." In the past, important affirmations of faith were often incorporated into the list of core values. Today, the complicated contexts of competing spiritualties demand more clarity about what faith affirmations members of a given church can be expected to share.

Bedrock beliefs are the faith convictions to which church members spontaneously turn for strength in times of trouble, stress, or confusion. These are the gut-level, heartfelt, bottom-line beliefs that help members endure and overcome the predicaments of life. Bedrock beliefs provide the basis of accountability for Christian hope in a world of cynicism and despair.

Again, I've taught this over and over again, and continue to be amazed at how difficult it is for church members and leaders to understand this. It's really quite simple. These are the deeply held faith convictions that members of the church community will predictably turn to for strength in times of trouble. Yet church people consistently make this complicated.

First, church members always want to *dogmatize* bedrock faith convictions. Faith becomes a matter of polity, policy, and intellectual assent. Church members imagine that doctrines of Creation, the Trinity, the Virgin Birth, the Authority of Scripture, or theories of Atonement are somehow "bedrock beliefs." In actual practice, however, in the midst of crisis (disease, accident, job loss, war, natural disaster, broken relationships, etc.) nobody automatically studies doctrine. They turn instead to a phrase of a hymn, a snippet of scripture, an icon of Christ, or a memory of grace that is beyond rationalization and doubt.

Second, church leaders always want to "theologize" bedrock faith convictions. Faith becomes an essay rather than a declaration. It becomes curriculum rather than an existential leap. Faith is lost in a fog of conflicting points of view or loses focus in an effable mystery that ends in absolute skepticism. If a seeker comes to church broken, lonely, lost, victimized, anxious, or afraid, there is no gospel to rescue them. A "theology" won't do

9

it. They need leaders who can speak articulately about their own spiritual victories and deepest convictions.

Bedrock beliefs are often expressed in specific, memorable, biblical verses. Church members find themselves repeating these verses at a significant life-cycle event (birth and baptism, marriage or divorce, death and funeral, etc.) Sometimes they are expressed through memorable words of the worship liturgy—particularly sacramental liturgy—or as specific verses from hymns. Church members find themselves singing (inwardly or outwardly) a lyrical phrase that uplifts their spirits or gives them courage to endure.

Biblical Expressions of Bedrock Beliefs	Liturgical Expressions of Bedrock Beliefs
The Lord is my shepherd! (Psalm 23)	*Our Father in heaven, hallowed by your name...*
But I know that my redeemer is alive! (Job 19:25)	*This is my body, broken for you.*
Don't fear because I am with you! (Isa 41:10)	*Jesus Christ, Son of God, have mercy on me a sinner.*
For where two or three are gathered in my name, I'm there with them. (Matt 18:20)	*Never be discouraged; take it to the Lord in prayer*
Ask and you will receive. Seek and you will find. (Luke. 1:9)	*You are giving and forgiving; ever blessing, ever blest...*
I am the bread of life! (John 6:35) I am the light of the world! (John 8:12)	*Like a mighty river flowing is the perfect peace of God*
Peace I leave with you. (John 14:27)	*Service is the golden cord, close binding humankind*
Nothing can separate us from God's love in Christ Jesus our Lord. (Rom 8:39)	*I am the Lord of the Dance...and I'll lead you all wherever you may be*
Now faith, hope, and love remain—these three things—and the greatest of these is love. (1 Cor 13:13)	*You breathe and there is health; you move and there is power*
If anyone is in Christ, that person is part of the new creation...new things have arrived! (2 Cor 5:17)	*The last shall be first and the weak shall be strong, and none shall be afraid*
Christ has set us free for freedom. (Gal 5:1)	*Omega and Alpha he! Let the organ thunder!*
For me, living serves Christ and dying is even better. (Phil 1:21)	*Amazing Grace! That saved a wretch like me...*

Be glad in the Lord always…the Lord is near. (Phil 4:4-5)	*O thirsty soul drink at the well; God's living water will never fail*
You must be doers of the word and not only hearers who mislead themselves. (James 1:22)	*Be still my soul, for God is on your side…*
Perfect love drives out fear. (1 John 4:18)	*Thirst quenched, soul revived, and now I live in him.*
Then I saw a new heaven and a new earth…. [God] will wipe away every tear from their eyes. (Rev 21:1-4)	*The love of God is broader than the measures of the mind; the heart of the eternal is most wonderfully kind.*

The verse may serve as key words that bring to memory an entire biblical story or a longer saying of Jesus. The lyric may trigger memories of a particular experience of public or private worship in which the believer feels closest to God.

- A bedrock belief is a conviction of faith to which people turn for strength in times of stress, confusion, or trouble. It's an automatic response of the soul to the struggles of living.

- A bedrock belief is the bottom-line confidence that allows Christians to hope for tomorrow. It is the way Christians confront the fundamental anxieties of emptiness, meaninglessness, fate, death, guilt, shame, and alienation.

- A bedrock belief is an act of courage. It is a church's stand against the threats of being lost, lonely, trapped, dying, broken, abused, or discarded.

One church, for example, translated the ancient faith convictions in the manner below. The beliefs are expressed in simple, dramatic language that any child to faith would readily understand.

- God's mercy in every situation…

- God's power when I can't…

- God's love when others don't…

- God's blessing not always seen…

11

- God's presence whether I feel it or not...

- God's companionship in the face of fear...

- God's grace no matter what happens...

- God's call when you don't know where you are going.

These are beliefs identified by a growing, urban Assemblies of God church, but they clearly don't reveal any specific or particular denominational agenda. These are beliefs that have a universal appeal to people with no Christian memory and are intended to draw people into an experience of Christ rather than platform or polity. Or, for another example:

- God is in control. (Rom 8:28)

- God forgives sins because of the sacrifice of Jesus Christ. (Col 1:14)

- Jesus is Lord. (Rom 14:9)

- Jesus is our example of a life that pleases the Father. (Eph 4:20-24; 1 Pet 2:21-22)

- The Holy Spirit empowers us to live in obedience to God. (Gal 5:21-25)

- The Bible is God's Word and is *the* final authority for all of life. (2 Tim 3:16)

- God hears and answers prayer. (1 John 5:14-15)

- We are children of God. (Rom 8:16-17)

These beliefs from an urban Baptist church are more doctrinal, partly because they have a clear conviction about the plain truth of scripture. The Midwestern, African American environment preserves a Christian memory in which these will still be readily understandable.

Core values and bedrock beliefs combine to shape the foundation of trust with which programs are implemented and creative ideas are initiated. *Without* this foundation of trust, it is extremely difficult to think strategically. The smallest change is controversial. Every program adjustment becomes political. *With* this foundation of trust, leaders can think strategically with less stress and greater speed.

Foundation of trust creates a culture of accountability. Today many churches are afraid of accountability because they think it will inevitably lead to judgmental and exclusive behavior. The exact opposite is true. Where there is no foundation of trust, there will only be endless competition and negotiation. And in the ensuing power struggle there will inevitably be judgment and exclusion. The culture of accountability is what builds confidence among members and credibility among publics. It creates the possibility for honesty and forgiveness, safety and hope.

Core values and bedrock beliefs may evolve over time, in different contexts, and in fresh experiences of grace. Churches often define, refine, and celebrate core values and beliefs at the same time they revisit their original vision (image and song) and mission statement. This is the basic function of an "annual meeting" for a small or midsized congregation. In larger churches, any congregational gathering for any purpose is an opportunity to proclaim, ponder, or celebrate the foundation of trust, and leaders are always careful that such gatherings include *more* than just food, fellowship, and an interesting program.

In any size church, worship is the primary way in which the foundation of trust is recognized and celebrated. We often think of worship solely as an opportunity to experience the immanence of the divine, but the *organizational* function of worship is to define, refine, and celebrate both the horizontal and vertical dimensions of trust. Core values and beliefs, may be presented through word, symbol, image, liturgical act, song, drama, and dance. If nothing else is taken away from worship, the clear memory of how we should live and why we should hope is crucial.

The foundation of trust becomes the *heartbeat* of congregational life. It is the pulse of the body of Christ. It is not always brought to consciousness, but it is always functioning. The heartbeat of values and beliefs is regular, universal, and consistent. When the body is under positive or negative stress, the *heartbeat* is faster. When the body is at rest, the heartbeat is slower. Yet it is the same heartbeat. If you could to take the pulse of every member and leader of the church, examining their daily lives, observing their spontaneous deeds at home or work, listening to their unrehearsed words the friends and neighbors, you would see the same core values and bedrock beliefs. Their hearts beat as one.

There can be no strategic thinking without consistently monitored, universally shared accountability for core values and bedrock beliefs.

Chapter 2
The Power of Strategic Thinking

Once the church creates a foundation of trust or culture of accountability, they can harness the power of strategic thinking. Trust is the essential ingredient for vision and mission. Vision always emerges from trust. Where there is no real trust, there can be no clear vision. The reason that so many churches are so vague and tentative about vision is that fundamentally they neither trust each other nor trust God.

Visions are revealed, not created. Churches inevitably get confused. They often think that visioning is some form of "brainstorming." It is not just that churches think visioning is an exercise of the *mind* but that it is accomplished by an exercise of the *will*. Church leaders think that if they just think harder, research more, sing more loudly, preach more powerfully, invent cleverer group activities, concentrate on the right talismans, shed more tears, beat their breasts black and blue, or imitate the best practices of "successful" churches that they are more likely to "get a vision."

The paradox of strategic thinking is that once you have created the foundation of trust, the incentive and motivation to strategically think at all comes from beyond the organization itself. You don't think up visions. You pray for visions. Or to say this another way, you open yourself to a "heartburst." The culture of accountability allows you to do that because your "heartbeat" is regular, universal, and consistent. Identity as a church is secure, and you can look beyond the church with confidence. Knowing *who* you are allows you to see others clearly. The publics out there are neither strangers who threaten you nor are they objects to be used for your survival. You can appreciate the unique value of the stranger, and God can open your heart to be generous to others.

Once again we see the value of intentional demographic and lifestyle research. We go beyond ourselves to see and understand the diversity of the publics. Our strategic thinking is guided not by what we want but by what others need. Since demographic trends and lifestyles experience are always changing, our vision is also changing. It needs to be prayerfully revisited every few years, because God may be calling us in a new direction to bless or serve different people.

Churches that are unable or unwilling to think strategically usually claim that visions are abstract, universal, and eternal. They say things like "Our vision is to multiply disciples of Christ"; or "Our vision is to bring peace and justice to the world"; or "Our vision is to be an authentic community of Christ welcoming all people." Such statements are recipes for inertia. Who exactly do you want to reach? What exactly do you want to do? Thinking they are called to reach everybody, they actually bless nobody. Thinking they are called to do everything, they actually do nothing.

In fact, visions are concrete, particular, and changing. A paradigm for visioning can be seen in the apostolic story of the mission to (and for, and with) the gentiles. Paul has a vision (Acts 16) of a Macedonian saying "Come over and help us!" His team stakes everything they have, takes enormous risks, and travels to where the Macedonian is. The Macedonians are a concrete and particular, definable and describable demographic. So Paul and his team listen, observe, adapt, and figure out how they can best help, serve, or bless the Macedonians. They spend months learning their customs, appreciating their food, listening to their music, and understanding their spirituality. Then, thinking strategically, they customize a ministry in unique ways for a unique people, to accomplish specific goals. And when they are successful, God reveals another vision of an Ephesian, or a Corinthian, or a Roman, or some other lifestyle segment emerging in the world.

Strategic thinking is motivated by, and aimed toward, the purpose of God to bless or serve somebody other than ourselves. What will that be? What blessing can we share, and what gift can we offer? And that purpose changes as society changes. This is why strategic thinking demands that every few years a church must refine and embed the foundation of trust all over again, prayerfully discern their vision all over again, and then figure out a way to change what they are doing to be more relevant to changing demographics.

All visions are simultaneously about *motivation* and *destination*. Visions motivate us because God shows us a particular public, and our heart breaks, bursts, and bubbles with a desire to bless, help, or serve them. Visions shape our goals because God reveals the potential outcome of a better, more hopeful life for and with them. Visions, therefore, are always emotional and metaphorical.

Strategic thinking is more art more than mechanics. Any great masterpiece begins with a vision that combines form, content, and significance in a unique way. The Spirit harnesses the mind of an artist and the body of an artist to create something that is at once *more* than the artist and *less* than perfect. God harnesses the best of a church to create an organization that is at once *more* than just an institution and *less* than the realm of God.

It begins with a picture that captures the soulful purpose of a church. An artist first visualizes the picture he wishes to create. That visualization is as much a revelation as a creation. It comes from the convergence of the artist's soul with the ideal of perfection. You might say (and most artists *do* say) that God is in the action just as much as the artist's ingenuity is.

The artist may then draw a pencil sketch, experiment with perspective and depth, reflect on tints and colors, and layer by layer create the picture. It may take a while. The artist may well erase work and start over again, or rework aspects of the picture, or touch up the painting with a miniscule adjustment that makes all the difference. Planning and implementation go hand in hand. Great art is always well conceived and expertly accomplished, but in the end it stands apart from the artist as a separate, living thing. The artist *did* it, and *didn't* do it at the same time.

Therefore, strategic thinkers often see themselves as artists. They are not just professionals (who happen to profess Christ) who bring their various educational, financial, or organizational skills to create task groups and budget lines. They visualize a picture that captures the soulful purpose of a church. They envision what the successful church will look like one, two, or perhaps ten years in the future standing amid the mission field. The picture is not a photo of the church building or membership; nor is it a landscape of the neighborhood's improved social fabric. It is truly a portrait in which a smiling church stands in the foreground, surrounded by a specially blessed mission field; and the observer readily imagines God somewhere above and beyond, laughing with delight.

The heart of a strategic thinker is the heart of an artist. Strategic thinkers need to be in touch with God. They need to open themselves to God's purpose of redemption and God's intention to mature the disciple and bless the stranger.

The step from vision discernment to strategic thinking is comparable to the design and construction of a cathedral. The architect is the artist who designs the sweep of the arches, the height of the spire, and the beauty of the windows. The cathedral is more than an ordinary building. It is a theological and missiological statement of identity and purpose, witness and message. The architect passes the concept to the engineers. The engineers do the calculations and create the blueprints. They set the priorities for construction so that the builders don't get ahead of themselves, paint themselves into a corner, or risk the whole construction falling to pieces. They distribute the weight, balance the elements, and create *usable space* out of *beautiful ideas*.

Three Ways to Define Vision

In order to render a vision concrete enough for construction, architects usually draw a sketch or build a model. Words alone are never enough. People need to see it in order to believe in it. They need to touch it in order to build it. Visions need to engage our senses of sight and touch, and even hearing, smell, and taste.

Similarly, strategic thinkers render a vision concrete in three different ways. Each incarnation of the vision guides church leaders to think strategically. Every time they revise the plan (add to the plan, perfect the plan, or alter the plan) they refer back to these three concrete renderings of the vision. This helps the plan stay aligned with the original intentions of God for the church.

Inspiring Image

Express the vision through an image—painting, watercolor, photo, or mural—that inspires anyone who looks at it. Many old churches include a large stained glass window, often above the chancel or altar, which communicates the identity and purpose of the church. The window may be of Christ the Good Shepherd, the Transfiguration, Jesus ascending into heaven, or other powerful images.

Most churches have a sanctuary or worship center, decorated in various traditional or contemporary ways. Most of the decorations and symbols are barely noticed by the regular participants and barely understandable by the visitors and seekers.

I remember one church in particular. It had a fairly modern sanctuary. It had flexible cathedral chairs, arching roof, skylight, pretty liturgical colors that nobody really understood, hardwood chancel furniture, and a cross. They used computer technology so that the words of songs, outlines of sermons, and various images of church life could be projected on side screens.

There was also a bare wall behind the pulpit made of red brick and glass block. It was actually freestanding, a partition behind which was the door to Sunday school rooms and washrooms. This bare wall was the first thing anybody saw entering the sanctuary. Since the curved rows of chairs always faced forward, the blank wall was the primary thing people stared at during and in between liturgical rites. If the preacher became boring, people stared at this wall. If the music stopped prematurely or people opened their eyes during prayer, they stared at this wall. True, they might stare at the cross, but when we surveyed successive worshiping congregations we learned that they didn't. The members didn't notice the cross because it was so commonplace, and the visitors didn't notice the cross because it didn't reveal anything specific about that particular church.

Therefore, the way to communicate the vision of the church was to paint a mural on that bare wall. This mural would have to be about 10 x 20 feet. It would be colorful, beautiful, eye-catching, and powerful. It would capture the heart, soul, and gut of what that church was all about. It would be the image of perfection toward which the church strived. It would reveal what anchored and motivated this particular church—out of all the other nice churches in the community.

When visitors or newcomers entered the sanctuary, the first thing they would see would be this mural, and they would instantly know the essence of this church. Nobody would need to explain it to them. They would see it right there in front of their eyes. The bulletin cover would have the same picture, and so also would the business card of the pastor, and the take-home gift from the welcome center. When they returned home and their spouse asked, "So, what was that church like?" they would instantly describe this picture.

When members entered the sanctuary, the first thing they would see would be this mural, and they would smile. They would come from busy lives, weary or restless, and one look at this mural would make them feel right at home. "Yes! That's us!" they would say. This is where I belong. This is what I am a part of. This is our dream and my dream, our journey and my journey, our hope and my hope. If someone at work ever asked them what their church was about, they would instantly describe this picture.

Of course, whether visitor or member, they would never be able to explain it fully. A picture is always worth a thousand words. And this mural would be so rich that every time someone looked at it, something new might appear. Yet it would always elicit joy—and demand to be shared with strangers.

What will that mural look like for your church? Leaders will take time to ponder and pray, to dialogue with church and community members, and to discern what that picture will be. They can invite church members who have special talents in painting or photography to create possibilities.

They can even invite the children of the Sunday school to draw with crayons and finger paint.

In the end, the church creates a veritable art gallery. They display these pictures for all to see. You can see similar themes and patterns emerge. The art of the children may inspire insights that the art of adults missed. Eventually, the church finds a consensus around a particular inspiring image. They may ask a professional graphics designer or a local community artist to create a mural or tapestry. The image will be highly visible inside and outside the church, and it will be used in all church communications. The gallery itself can be placed on their website.

Here are some examples that might be inspiring—and some hints about how later strategic thinking aligned to reveal and pursue the vision.

Phoenix Rising

This urban core church has a huge tapestry of a contemporary phoenix rising from the ashes of the city. The phoenix, of course, is an ancient Christian symbol for the resurrection. The bird is depicted soaring above the city, wings embracing the skyline. The points of flame are the skyscrapers, apartment buildings, and slums; and the ashes below are clearly discernible human beings walking, running, catching taxis, and even fighting and arguing. The phoenix rises from the ashes toward a glowing sun.

The tactics that aligned to the vision included demolition of the heritage Gothic cathedral building and the erection of an eleven-story high-rise with housing for newly arrived immigrants. The church initiated career counseling, ESL (English as a Second Language) teaching, job placement programs, and many other services aimed especially at refugees who had left behind everything, even loved ones, to find a new life.

The tapestry was commissioned from a local artist who lived in the same downtown core. It eventually became an enormous banner suspended from the building outside and was the symbol on every letter or flyer issued from the church.

Whatever their tactics might be, the *motivation* and *destination* are clear. For whom does their heart burst? It bursts for immigrants, refugees, and anyone whose life is in ashes. Where do they want to end up? They foresee a church as a way station, which desperate people enter to find help and exit with new hope.

Angels in Our Midst

This country church has a large triptych (three-panel mural) painted on the wall behind the pulpit. The sanctuary itself is very plain and traditional, but the entire back wall reveals three ten-foot angels. These are not modern cupids or sweetly smiling young men or women. These are biblical messengers—at once stern, compassionate, and far-seeing. One carries a trumpet, one a sword, and the third raises a hand in blessing. Each stands in the foreground of a rural scene (cornfield, village, and farm). Some newcomers are surprised (and occasionally alarmed) when they first enter the church and see these towering figures, but they are soon reassured. They create an atmosphere of confidence and safety.

The tactics that aligned to the vision included local organic markets, global outreach to address hunger, employment counseling, seniors housing, personal and business financial planning, prayer circles, annual blessing of the animals, and anything that touched the stressful lives of the declining rural life of America. The mission was clear: "Guardian Angels for Our Communities." We will be guardian angels of our communities. We will bring hope, safety, and vindication to people in need.

The triptych was obviously painted by talented amateurs within the congregation. They are good, but occasionally you see that the perspective is awry or the color is inconsistent. That only adds to the authenticity of the vision. Working people labored on this and believe in its message.

Whatever their tactics might be, the *motivation* and *destination* are clear. For whom does their heart burst? It bursts for rural families struggling to make a living and sustain healthy relationships. Where do they want to end up? They foresee a church that protect the rights of women and children, and any who are left behind by society, bringing justice and hope to an entire county.

Multicultural Jesus

This exurban church has a floor-to-ceiling, wall-to-wall painting of Jesus in a fishing boat. The surrounding disciples are clearly from every nation or culture on earth. The fishing net flows out of the boat into a turbulent sea, but in the center of the boat are the simple loaves and fishes described in the Gospel. Jesus and all the disciples are young, rough, muscular fishermen; and they are all facing outward with remarkable expressions of welcome, anticipation, and joy.

The tactics that aligned to the vision included worship in multiple languages, shared facilities with other Christian churches, small group multiplication, sidewalk Sunday schools, evangelistic rock concerts, mission teams to disaster zones, and other ministries that were all done in a deliberately cross-cultural way. The mission statement was simple: "Get in the boat!" It was an invitation and a command all at once. Are you lost? Get in the boat! Are you only nominally Christian? Get in the boat! Fellowship and service are one.

The painting is likely an enlarged print of a more famous work (since the credit is below it), but it is no less the heart and soul of the church. This is actually not in the sanctuary (since for architectural reasons there was no room to prominently display it). Instead it hangs on the wall beside the entrance, dominating the narthex where the refreshments are served and the people gather.

Whatever their tactics might be, the *motivation* and *destination* are clear. For whom does their heart burst? It bursts for every ethnicity and race in the multicultural neighborhood. Where do they want to end up? They foresee a church membership that mirrors the cultural diversity of the neighborhood, in which fellowship and service go hand in hand.

These are all inspirational examples. Just to describe them is exciting. Imagine what it would feel like to see the images vividly, boldly, and regularly. Against these pictures, strategic thinkers can compare every program and budget line of the church.

Theme Song

Express the vision through music—a combination of words and lyric. In the past, many churches identified favorite hymns that expressed in poetry the identity and purpose of the church. Songs may be traditional or contemporary, in any genre, accompanied by any instrumentation. They function like

- a national anthem that is sung with united enthusiasm on special occasions;

- a university "fight song" that inspires the crowd and energizes their team to score; or

- a marching cadence that sustains weary pilgrims to continue their journey.

Imagine such a song that could be sung in every worship service and could begin every board meeting or congregational gathering. Members will hum the song when jogging, walking, or exercising at the gym. They may sing it quietly either in meditation or during housework.

A theme song usually has memorable lyrics that can be memorized by young and old. It has a strong rhythm that wakes people up and restores their energy. It expresses clearly Christian content that causes people to focus on God (Father, Son, and/or Holy Spirit).

A theme song reveals the core values and beliefs that are special to the church. It motivates volunteer commitment and sacrificial service. It sharply defines the purpose of the church and their reason for existence in a particular community. The soundtrack is on the website. For example:

- Phoenix Place, the church described earlier with the image of a phoenix rising, was especially committed to empathizing with and supporting refugees and newly arrived immigrants. Many had left families and careers at home, and now were trying to start a new life. Their theme song was chosen from the denominational hymn-book and is called "From the Slave Pens of the Delta," by Herbert O'Driscoll.

- A new church development ("church plant") in a new neighborhood with young couples and young families chose the well-known song: "The Lord of the Dance" by Sydney Carter. The song fit well with their inspiring image of the "Laughing Jesus." Its strong rhythm and memorable refrain inspired adults in worship and young children in the Sunday school, and it suited their informal worship in the gym of a public school.

- An older, African American church in the urban core especially empathized with the poor and unemployed, and young adults who were addicted to drugs and violence. The church building housed numerous social services, including medical clinics and addiction intervention groups. They had a strong youth ministry to provide a safe haven from street gangs. They chose the historic song "Amazing Grace" with the original lyrics of John Newton. Whenever they sang the phrase "that saved a wretch like me," the entire congregation would shout out the words as loud as they could.

- Yet another church in an affluent neighborhood encouraged their music director to compose an entirely new song. The worship was highly liturgical, and they had the resources of a very talented choir. This song was copyrighted and recorded for use beyond the congregation by various local micro-charities and global missionaries, and is available on their website.

- A house church reaching out to blue-collar young adults, and single parents with young children made an unusual choice: "I'm on My Way," written and recorded by the Scottish folk/pop group The Proclaimers and popularized in the Disney movie *Shrek*. The members delighted in playing the song as loud as possible when driving their pickup trucks to work. The recording was played every Sunday to summon the members from the coffee room to the sanctuary for worship.

Notice how each of these songs connect with the lifestyle groups surrounding the church. The words and lyrics, genres and instrumentations all suit the daily habits of the people they long to reach. What is your song? What is the song that captures the vision of your congregation in your neighborhood or community?

Mission Statement

Only after a church has chosen an inspiring image and a song in the heart do they attempt to write a mission statement. Many churches ignore these first steps, and their mission statements are too complicated and rarely memorable. Their statements may be generic to a denomination or sound too programmatic and institutional. The publics don't seek an institution in which to belong but a movement of the Spirit in which to participate. Charitable givers are not generous toward institutions with high overhead and low motivation but give generously to churches with big, bold visions—even when their ambitions are expensive.

There are so many misunderstandings about mission statements. In order to understand what a great mission statement looks like, it is often helpful to identify three common mistakes churches make.

- A mission statement is NOT about institutional survival. It's not about keeping the doors open or preserving a denomination. God's purpose for the church is always about multiplying disciples and blessing the world.

- A mission statement is NOT a brief summary of all the programs. It's not an index of our committees. It's about *who* we strive to bless and *how* we strive to bless them.

- A mission statement is NOT a theological essay. It is not a historical overview. It is everything a seeker needs to know about why this church is important for the diverse people on the west side of Las Vegas.

I've consulted and traveled among churches all over the country. Every thriving, effective church in America can summarize their purpose with a *handful* of carefully chosen words, a logo or image that can be printed on the side of a bus, and a theme song celebrated in every worship service.

A great mission statement is brief, memorable, and energizing. When you think strategically, it is printed at the top of the page. Immediately following the mission statement will be five to ten measureable outcomes with which the church will evaluate its success in accomplishing the mission. The mission statement for every thriving church is different. But they all have certain elements in common.

A great mission statement is

- clearly motivational: The mission statement is exciting to people in both church and community, and it is regularly celebrated by the congregation as the unique way in which they follow Jesus. The mission energizes people. It is a source of pride. Members readily speak of it among work associates, neighbors, relatives, and friends.

- clearly congregational: The mission statement is the sum of congregational life, and not simply one program of the church. Every member is enthusiastic and wholehearted about that mission. Each person is "on fire" for that mission, and they participate in this congregation specifically because these people are working toward that purpose.

- utterly distinctive: The mission statement uses words or metaphors unique to that particular congregation in their unique demographic context. It distinguishes the purpose of this congregation from the unique missions of other churches even in the same denomination.

- profoundly sacrificial: No matter how large the vision or how great the challenge, a powerful mission statement is always reasonable and achievable. It deserves immense personal sacrifice. It will be used effectively in all stewardship campaigns and nominations processes.

- always prayerful: Individuals, leaders, and the congregation as a whole continually pray for the success of the mission. Prayer is both planned and spontaneous. The mission is constantly lifted into consciousness, and it lies at the center of personal and corporate spirituality.

Your ultimate goal will be to articulate your mission in such a way that it can be easily printed on the side of a bus, on a park bench, or on a banner trailing behind an airplane above the city. In that brief space, you need to communicate everything necessary to capture the imagination of the public and motivate enormous sacrifice by church members.

Visions are expressed in images, songs, and then words. Postmodern people are like ancient people in that they learn more through sensory inputs than abstract symbols. Perhaps this is because literacy is actually declining, and people are watching more videos, listening to more music, and owning more electronic devices than ever before. Pictures and songs capture the heart of a church more powerfully than any sermon, treatise, book, or curriculum.

Consensus is crucial. It is impossible to think strategically without a picture to capture the breadth and depth of the vision, and without a song to express the urgency and power of the vision, and without a brief, punchy statement to communicate instantly the supreme value of the vision. If there is no concrete rendering of the heart, soul, and aspiration of a church *as a whole*, then vision will inevitably shift to focus the vision on the self-interests of a particular controlling individual or faction.

There is always a picture. The question is whether it is *our* picture or *my* picture. If it is only *my* picture, then planning will quickly break down into competing factions vying for pet projects and personal agendas. *My* picture will compete with *your* picture—and every other person's picture—and the only thing that keeps a planning process from open warfare is parliamentary procedure.

Yet parliamentary procedure is in itself *a picture*! It is a picture of a ballot box and hands in the air, and a mission statement declaring, "The ayes have it!" It is a story of debate, compromise, and the lowest common denominator. It is a picture of contented people accomplishing little. Try painting *that* picture on the back wall of your sanctuary. See how many visitors and newcomers return. See how many members smile with anticipation. It's a human picture, but it's not God's picture. It has emerged from the give and take of politics but not the prayerful intersection of human yearning and divine purpose that is the source of true vision.

However, the vision is defined, it reveals the true "Heart Song" of the church. The "Heart Beat" (consistency and consensus of core values and beliefs) creates an opportunity for God to reveal the Heart Song that motivates and guides everyone and everything in the church.

After all is said and done, and after all the costs of discipleship have been weighed, the final question is always one of alignment. Does each particular tactic *align* perfectly with the vision or not? Look at the picture. Sing the song. Look at the tactic. Is there a direct line connection? Or is there some measure of doubt? That urban core church, for example, will always ask of any new idea or enduring program: *Is it a "Phoenix" thing to do?* The country church will ask: *Is it perfectly obvious that we are on the side of the angels?* The exurban church will ask: *Does this tactic get more people "in the boat" or "on board" with Christ"?* In a time of limited resources, churches don't want to do things that only "sort of" align with vision. If something doesn't align with the vision, then we don't do it. If it does align perfectly with the vision, then we must do it.

Whether the vision is captured on canvass, set to music, or defined in words, it is the Heart Song that emerges from the Heart Beat of trust in God and accountability in membership. It motivates churches to soar on the wings of the Spirit to touch the lives of particular publics.

Chapter 3

The Way of Strategic Thinking: The Path of the Board

O nce the church builds a foundation of trust and discerns a power-ful vision, they can follow a path of strategic thinking. Strategy emerges from vision, because vision forces the church to define measure-able outcomes. The church must be able to see progress (or regress) con-cretely. They must be able to decide who will lead and who will be blessed; and what, when, and how they will act to pursue God's vision. They must be able to measure the cost of discipleship and anticipate the stress of inevitable change.

Churches that sustain effective ministries regularly follow a specific path of strategic thinking. It's as essential as an annual physical examina-tion with a doctor, an annual maintenance schedule for an automobile, or an annual review of financial investments. Regularity and consistency are important. People are tempted by laziness and inattention to assume "everything is all right for another year" and live to regret their lack of discipline. There are several reasons why regularity and consistency are important.

First, the mission field is changing constantly, and strategies that were relevant one year may be a sidetrack the next. Even small changes in de-mographic trends, lifestyle preferences, or physical and spiritual needs can make a big difference in the speed of church growth and the impact of congregational mission.

Second, the routine of strategic thinking keeps the foundation of trust as a primary vehicle for accountability. The positive experience of membership growth actually carries the hidden liability that core values, beliefs, vision, and mission may somehow be diluted or altered. Even veteran members are still sinners, and pride and self-interest all too easily supplant mission impact in the programming and budgeting of a church.

Third, the consistency of strategic thinking allows the benefits to be cumulative. The habits of continuous learning, evaluation, strategic adjustment, and risk taking mature a congregation over the years. It keeps leaders sharp and church members faithful. The more you do it, the more you mature from it, and the congregational reputation for effectiveness grows in the community.

The method unfolds in two parallel paths and involves staff, board, and ministry teams. The first stage (described in this chapter) is the work of the board. They focus on community research, spiritual discernment, and comparative insights between the church and the mission field. The second stage (described in the next chapter) is the work of ministry teams. They focus on assessing the effectiveness of ministries, triage that identifies flagging or irrelevant ministries, and creative new ideas. In practice, the senior staff and board tend to focus on community research and lead the entire congregation in spiritual discernment; and the program staff and ministry team leaders tend to focus on church assessment. Their insights come together in a leadership summit.

This is the way of strategic thinking. Although the information, issues, priorities, and leadership teams change, the process itself is deliberately repetitive. It becomes *routine* for the church. It becomes more and more familiar. At the beginning, it may seem burdensome and depressing, but over time it becomes easily manageable and increasingly exciting. After all, the point of strategic thinking is to boldly go where God wants them be, and to risk all for the sake of God's mission.

Community Research

Strategic thinking occurs at the intersection of listening to God and listening to the public. That is the crucible in which Christian ministry is refined like gold, the treasure of great worth in any church. The immediacy of Jesus Christ meets the urgency of spiritual yearning. Church leaders want to place themselves right there, in the middle of that intersection, where the sparks fly and the tears flow and lives are changed and shaped forever.

The board (including the pastor) and ministry team leaders (including paid and unpaid) each play a part in strategic thinking. Boards are mainly concerned with aligning the church with vision and mission, networking in the community, long-term and big picture thinking, and measuring overall outcomes for success. Ministry team leaders are mainly concerned with the integrity and effectiveness of programs, equipping volunteers, and short-term or annual implementation.

Clearly, the work of the board and ministry team leaders overlaps. Occasionally the board will want to focus on a particular program during the leadership summit, even though ministry team leaders believe it is functioning very well at the moment. Future changes in the community may bring fresh challenges for programming. And occasionally the ministry team leaders will want to focus on mission alignment because new ideas require some course corrections. Every five years or so, a church will want to spend more time and attention on strategic thinking precisely because these overlaps deserve discussion.

Nevertheless, the primary role of the board in strategic thinking is research. The primary role of ministry team leaders is assessment. These two roles come together to help the church make wise decisions that will accelerate church growth and positively impact the community.

The Contemporary Situation

Not long ago, church growth apparently depended on the principle of homogeneity. The church members all resembled each other and represented a single demographic (ethnicity, race, economic status, etc.). Church participation included a relatively small number of lifestyle segments who were clearly compatible with each other. It wasn't difficult to analyze the community either, because communities and neighborhoods were also pretty uniform. People were less mobile, and average residency was ten years or higher. There was no Internet. People shopped in local stores, commuted short distances to work, and spent holidays at the park.

The situation is reversed today, though the reversal began before most current church leaders were alive. Church growth depends on heterogeneity. The goal of a healthy church is not to be separate from the community but to mirror the diversity of the community. Church members don't all look alike. Their unity depends on shared core values and bedrock beliefs but not on unanimous agreement about politics and public policies or local customs and social mores. It is far more difficult to analyze the community because people are more diverse. Ideas are shaped by the Internet and social media. People are incredibly mobile. While average residency for many established church members might be fifteen years or more, average residency in the community may only be six months. People shop in big-box stores miles away, commute long distances to work, and holiday in other countries.

In the days of homogeneity, the church often saw itself in *confrontation* with culture. Today the church must necessarily be in *conversation* with culture.

This is why church growth and community development are now two sides of the same coin. The church (or any spiritual organization) will not grow unless it helps the community develop; and the community will not develop unless the churches (or spiritual organizations) thrive. The church helps shape the social values and sustainable living of the community; and the community helps shape the vision and relevance of the church. The Holy Spirit is not only present in the church but also in the community. Jesus the Christ is not only present in the church programs but ahead of the church doing new things to bless the surrounding publics. The challenge to the church is not only to shape relevant programs for ministry today but to catch up with Jesus who is already doing creative new things for the future.

Demographic and Lifestyle Research

Demographic research is actually a set of "progressive lenses" that allows church leaders to explore demographic trends, lifestyle behaviors, and the moods and values of diverse publics. In the past, demographic research primarily concentrated on the community alone. It wasn't used to explore the diversity of the church because church members were pretty much all alike. Today the diversity within the church must be compared and contrasted with the diversity beyond the church. Church leaders need to know what lifestyles are over- or underrepresented in church membership when compared to the community.

At the moment, the only dynamic tool that allows church leaders to compare and contrast membership to mission field is www.MissionInsite.com.[2] There is a wealth of information here.

However, leaders need only to research specific things.

- trends, behavior patterns, and ministry expectations in the community
- trends, behavior patterns, and ministry relevance in the church

They can then compare and contrast these insights for the purposes of strategic thinking. They will be able identify

- how church programs need to evolve, adapt, and change
- how change will raise the stress level for church members

Leaders can then assess ongoing programs. They can make wise decisions to improve existing programs, initiate creative ideas, and terminate ineffective tactics with greater confidence and objectivity. They can anticipate stress and help church leaders accept changes on behalf of the greater mission of God through the church.

The demographic search engine www.MissionInsite.com is the most dynamic tool available specifically for churches today. In the past, churches could only study census data that was upgraded slowly and was nearly incomprehensible to ordinary people. At least 80 percent of the data was useless, and the rest was subject to so many interpretations as

---

2. You can also reach MissionInsite at miinfo@missioninsite.com.

to be next to useless. Now churches can study data from a variety of national, municipal, nonprofit, and corporate sources, which are updated monthly or annually. The data not only provides statistics but also insights in community attitudes and lifestyle behaviors. Most importantly, MissionInsite is a dynamic tool that allows you to define your own search parameters, explore current trends and cultural benchmarks, and customize reports directly relevant for effective ministry.

At the present moment most major denominations subscribe to it and make it available to their congregations. About one-third of all the churches in the United States can access it. If your denomination doesn't have access, you can subscribe as an individual congregation for a small fee. This is the search engine I will have in my mind as I explain the following steps for research.

Of course, there are many ways you can research your mission field. There will be many specific questions or issues you will want to address, and these may take you to any number of tools to do it. However, there are typically twelve steps in the basic research undertaken by a board to prepare for a leadership summit.

People Plot

In order to compare and contrast members to mission field, the church must upload their membership list (name and location) in the search engine. This is called "People Plot" in MissionInsite. There are instructions to do this, and if a church membership tracking software can be converted to a Microsoft Excel file (as most are) it is relatively easy.

The locations of all church members will appear as red dots on the computer screen. There are more advanced features that can also allow you to identify the locations of adherents, first- and second-time visitors, and membership status (transfer of membership, affirmation of faith, etc.). These will appear as different color dots on the screen.[3] As we shall see, the physical location of members will reveal a great deal about lifestyle representation and ministry expectations within the membership and help us

---

3. In the near future, there will be additional customizable People Plot attributes available including text, numeric, and date attribute fields.

contrast this to ministry expectations among different lifestyle segments in the community.

Once People Plot is created for the first time, it's quite easy for the church secretary to update it regularly. The secretary can supply the board and ministry teams with printed reports at any time in the year, research specific demographic trends or lifestyle expectations, and target mailings to specific households (e.g., first-time visitors or people who have moved into a neighborhood within the last six months).

It's important to note that churches can also upload and track household financial giving. This information can be limited to only trusted administrators to protect confidentiality. It will be invaluable down the road when leaders assess the real cost of changing programs or initiating creative ideas, because the board can know the real financial potential of the church without guesswork.

Search Area

Comparative research requires that the church define the parameters of a specific search area. In MissionInsite there are various tools with which the search area can be drawn.

- Radius search areas help leaders get a general idea of church and community trends but are less helpful for annual planning.

- Freehand search areas are especially drawn using north/south/east/west boundaries of streets and roads, utilities, school districts, or key geographic realities (like lakes, rivers, and mountains) that shape travel patterns.

- Travel Polygons guide the system to automatically draw a search area by car travel or walking in distance or time. This is often the most helpful search area because it can be adjusted to match the average commute of church members to regular worship.

The search area can easily be edited so that the shape can include or exclude particular neighborhoods or clusters of church members. In preparation for the annual leadership summit, the board may give explicit instructions to redraw a search area.

There are two distinct ways that these tools can be used. Leaders need to understand the current "Reach" and Depth" of the congregation based on People Plot.

- The current "Reach" of a congregation is revealed by a polygon drawn to include at least 75–80 percent of the congregational households in the People Plot. This not only reveals the geographical spread of church members but also the specific directions in which the church is growing, and even the travel routes that make the church site most accessible.

- The current "Depth" of a congregation is revealed by the "Heat Map" option when viewing People Plot. The Heat Map highlights the highest population densities of member households. The search area drawn around these "hot spots" of church membership includes a smaller percentage of members but often reveals the locations where churches have the most attraction or influence in any given neighborhood.

These two methods help leaders discern potential for volunteer recruitment, fund-raising, alternative sites of ministry, marketing strategies, and other helpful information.

Thematic Map

A thematic map reveals population density throughout the primary mission field and highlights specific neighborhoods or regions by color and code. These maps can be saved as JPEG images and transferred to printed documents or PowerPoint slides. These are extremely valuable before, during, and after the leadership summit to help ministry teams understand diversity at a glance.

The one thematic map that is most useful is the Mosaic Map. *Mosaic* is the term used to describe lifestyle segment diversity. Currently there are seventy-one distinct lifestyle segments in America (in nineteen lifestyle groups), each of which encompasses a group of people with distinct tastes and attitudes; behavior patterns; and expectations of church leaders, programs, and technologies.[4]

---

4. This data is from Experian (www.Experian.com), which is a global information service that operates in at least forty countries. Among other research, Experian tracks the digital "footprints" of people revealed through credit card use and other digital behavior.

The Mosaic Map, therefore, provides a visual display of population density by lifestyle segment. Each has a specific code, and a legend identifies the name of each lifestyle segment. When the Mosaic Map is combined with People Plot, leaders can also visualize the kind of people with whom specific households have particular affinities. "Birds of a feather flock together." People tend to live among neighbors with whom they are most comfortable.

Eventually, this will allow leaders to compare and contrast lifestyle representation between church membership and mission field. It will also provide valuable information about how programs need to be adapted to follow demographic trends or bless particular lifestyle segments.

Phase of Life

The broadest overview of church membership and mission field is revealed by studying "Phase of Life." This blends information about age and lifecycle. When church people refer to children, youth, adults, or seniors (for example), leaders must ask *which particular* groups they mean. Today there is enormous diversity among age groups.

MissionInsite allows leaders to build their own report (rather than just download a predefined report that contains extraneous information). This table can be transferred to an Excel file for distribution and study.

Phase of Life	Today	Ten Years Ahead
Before Formal Schooling: Ages 0 to 4		
Requiring Formal Schooling: Ages 5 to 19		
College/Career Starts: Ages 20 to 24		
Singles and Young Families: Ages 25 to 34		
Families and Empty Nesters: Ages 35 to 54		
Enrichment Years Singles/ Couples: Ages 55 to 64		
Retirement Opportunities 65+		

This table helps leaders see basic community trends today and for the next ten years. How does it help? For example, a common suburban pattern today is that the life phase of households with children ages 0 to 4 is growing (widespread, mini-baby boom), while the life phase of households with children ages 5 to 19 is declining. This might cause leaders to shift program emphases from Sunday school and youth programs to day care and parenting classes. It might suggest an expansion and upgrade to their nursery, along with a capital campaign to do it. Or it might mean removing some rear pews to make room for bassinets and strollers during worship.

Another common pattern in the exurbs, for example, is that the life phase for families and empty nesters is slowly declining, while the life phase for college and career starts (ages 20 to 24+) and for enrichment opportunities (ages 55 to 64) is growing. This might warn church leaders to expect more difficulty in finding volunteer leaders and board members (who are often recruited from among empty-nesters); and encourage them to increase worship options and contemporize music styles for singles and young couples living large on shoestring budgets and alienated from church institutions.

Comparative Lifestyle Representation

The most valuable predefined report uniquely available through MissionInsite is the ComparativeInsite Report. Leaders can directly compare membership to mission field. It is created from the parameters of the search area you have defined and the People Plot that is visible within that area. The computer automatically provides leaders with the following data:

Total Congregants		Total No. of Mosaic Segments in Study Area	
Total Congregant Household		Total No. of Mosaic Segments with Congregant Households Present	
Total Population in Study Area			
Total Households in Study Area		Estimated Household Penetration Rate	

You may want to adjust the search area so that it includes at least 75–80 percent of the church members (congregants) and reflects the significant diversity of lifestyles (mosaic segments) that is the Reach of the church. Alternatively, you may want to adjust the search area as a "Heat Map" that reflects the significant density of church presence and influence in a smaller area. Either way, you will immediately see the total number of people and households in the area. If the population is significantly higher than households, then the number of individuals in each household is *growing*. You can explore further to discover if expanding households means more children; returning young adults (often called "boomerangs") forced to live at home while looking for stable employment; or perhaps aging seniors moving closer to stores, transportation, and health care.

The estimated household penetration rate provides a marker revealing how successfully the church is connecting with people in that search area. The value of this is really cumulative. Over the years, leaders can see if church presence in an area is growing or declining.

Comparative Lifestyle Expectation

The ComparativeInsite Report directly compares and contrasts lifestyle representation for church membership and mission field. Both the actual number of households and the percentage of lifestyle representation are listed according to size (largest to smallest) for the study area.

As a rule of thumb, the top 50–70 percent of lifestyle segments defines the culture of a community or church. In the community, the top 50–70 percent shapes the retail, school system, health care, emergency services, transportation priorities, and other aspects of culture. In the church, the top 50–70 percent shape the hospitality, worship, education, small group, outreach, and other program emphases; and it shapes expectations for facilities, technologies, stewardship, and communication methodologies.

In the example below, you can see that the primary mission field included 574 church members (congregants), in a study area of 213,391 people. Comparison of population to household suggests that households on average contain 1–2 persons. There are 61 different lifestyle segments, of which 37 are represented in the congregation. Over the years, leaders can see if the penetration rate becomes more or less than 0.4 percent.

Comparative Mosaic Segment Report							
Total Congregants		574		Total No. of Mosaic Segments in Study Area			61
Total Congregant Households		326		Total No. of Mosaic Segments with			
Total Population in Study Area		213,391		Congregant HH Present			37
Total Households in Study Area		82,767		Estimated Household Penetration Rate			0.4%

		Study Area		Congregation		Analysis	
Mosaic Codes	**Mosaic Segment**	**2015**	**2015 %**	**Cong HH**	**Cong HH %**	**Index**	**Pen Rate**
O54	Striving Single Scene	9,775	11.8%	10	3.1%	26	0.1%
H26	Progressive Potpourri	6,900	8.3%	28	8.6%	104	0.4%
I33	Balance and Harmony	4,942	6.0%	15	4.6%	77	0.3%
I32	Steadfast Conventionalists	4,358	5.3%	4	1.2%	23	0.1%
C11	Aging of Aquarius	4,191	5.1%	18	5.5%	108	0.4%
L42	Rooted Flower Power	4,088	4.9%	23	7.1%	145	0.6%
O51	Digital Dependents	3,654	4.4%	6	1.8%	41	0.2%
B07	Generational Soup	3,290	4.0%	35	10.7%	268	1.1%

The top 50–70 percent of lifestyle segments in this example is included in the table above. You quickly see that lifestyle segments O51 and O54, and I32 and I33, are *under*represented in the church; and segments L42 and B07 are significantly *over*represented in the church. If church leaders adjust programs to focus on the former segments, they can anticipate stressful reactions from the latter segments.

But just what are the expectations for various ministry programs within each lifestyle segment? And how are they different? MissionInsite provides a commentary on all 71 lifestyle segments and 19 lifestyle groups describing in detail their ministry expectations.[5] The resource is called *Mission Impact Guide*. Expectations are sorted in the following categories, within which are specific alternatives.

---

5. These commentaries were created based on my wide and long experience as a consultant, the critique and guidance of regional and local church colleagues, and especially on the lifestyle descriptions developed by the multinational corporation Experian. Experian gathers and sorts vast amounts of digital information to create, name, and describe lifestyles for planners in education, health, social service, business, government, and other sectors.

Leadership Blend no more than two leadership functions or identities at any given time	Caregiver	Merciful, compassionate; special training in pastoral care and counseling; strong visitor; on call 24/7. Usually Ordained.
	Enabler	Approachable facilitator; special training in generational ministries; sensitive to lifestyle cycles; committed to tradition. Usually Ordained.
	CEO	Organizer, fund raiser; manages staff & volunteers; coordinates programs; excellent communicator. Ordained with administrative experience.
	Faith Tutor (Discipler)	Discipler with explicitly Christian perspective: Strong spiritual habits; matures Christians, grows leaders, mobilizes teams; strong seeker sensitivity, high accountability. Ordained or Lay.
	Guru (Discipler)	Discipler with broadly spiritual perspective: Strong spiritual habits; respect for multiple faith traditions; grows individuals, empowers spiritual life; provides enlightenment and encourages serenity.
	Visionary	Strategic and long-term planner; strong motivator; cross-sector credibility; serious spiritual habits and discernment. Ordained or Lay.
	Mentor	Penetrating intuition, extreme spiritual discipline; 1:1 focus on incarnational experience to break addictions and focus personal mission. Lay or neo-Monastic.
	Pilgrim	Accountable spiritual life, cross-cultural journey; "priestly" persona, inter-faith insights; radical sacrifice and simplicity. Lay or neo-Monastic.
Hospitality Blend no more than two hospitality options at any given time	The Basics	One size fits all. One layer of untrained greeters; limited availability of generic foods; single serving station; no goodbyes.
	Multiple Choices	Different strokes for different folks. Layers of trained greeters, focus on newcomers. Ongoing food court. Immediate follow-up.
	Healthy Choices	Targeted hospitality. Layers of trained greeters; board or small group leaders intentionally mingle; health, allergy conscious foods. Small group invitations.
	Take-Out	Mobile hospitality. Designated roving greeters; take food into worship, and take food home from church. Digital, wireless communication; follow up tweets and texts.

Worship Blend no more than two worship options at any given time	Educational Worship	Bless people with information, interpretation, exposition, explanation, and advocacy. Link to tradition, take notes, and watch the clock. Words; aim at the head.
	Transformation Worship	Bless people with personal change & divine intervention. Rescue the trapped and addicted. Stories, drama, action, rhythm. Role models; aim at the gut.
	Inspirational Worship	Bless people with high spirits and light hearts. Sing, applaud, shout, enjoy, and send people fearless and strong into the world. Images; aim at the heart.
	Coaching Worship	Bless people with practical help to live a Christian lifestyle at home, work, and play; informal, relational, and "how to." Video, drama, expertise. Aim at behavior.
	Healing	Bless people with physical, mental, relational, spiritual healing. Prayer, rites, awesome silence. Chants, background music, sensory experience. Aim at the body.
	Caregiving	Bless people with belonging. Pass the peace, children's stories, classic hymns, pastoral prayers, traditions. Gentle reminders, positive vibes. Aim at continuity.
	Mission-Connection Worship	Bless people with opportunities to covenant for mission; celebrate mission results. Cross-cultural, international, simultaneous witness & social service. High-tech.
Education Form Preference for one option over another	Curricular	Children, youth, and adult education are oriented around printed books or study guides. Passive, intellectual, classroom. Maturity measured by acquired knowledge.
	Experiential	Children, youth, and adult education are oriented around activities. More music, images, movement, interaction. Maturity measured by behavior patterns, attitudes.
Education Content Preference for one option over another	Biblical	Content focuses on the Old and New Testaments (and ancient Christian literature); interpreted historically, culturally, and doctrinally. Maturity means biblical literacy.
	Topical	Content concerning contemporary issues, ethical principles, or comparative religions. Faith applied to daily events. Maturity means ethical integrity and enlightened behavior.
Education Grouping Preference for one option over another	Generational	Gathers people by age, and parallel the grades of the public school system. Each age or grade to have private space and age-appropriate resources.
	Peer Group	Gather people by affinity or special interest, parallels the friendship circles that are "extracurricular" to the public school. Common enthusiasm, multipurpose space.

Small Group Leaders Preference for one option over another	Rotated Leaders	Participants take turns leading the group. Leaders are primarily fellowship hosts and conversation facilitators. Limited training.
	Designated Leaders	Single leader guides the group from start to finish. Leaders are chosen for spiritual maturity and guide spiritual growth. Significant training.
Small Group Form Preference for one option over another	Curriculum	Focus on a book, workbook, or structured program; chosen by the group or leader. The outcome of group participation is greater knowledge or self-awareness.
	Affinity	Focus on shared interest, enthusiasm, or activity. Personal growth occurs in the midst of the affinity, and the outcome is healthy behavior or mission.
Outreach Preferences to *receive* ministry may be different from preferences to *share* ministry Multiple preferences are possible	Survival	Focus on basic needs for food, shelter, clothing, employment, and basic health care. Often related to food banks, shelters, recycling, job placement, and medical clinics.
	Recovery	Focus on addiction intervention, 12-step support, and counseling. Often address addictions (alcohol, drugs, tobacco, gambling, and pornography, and more).
	Health	Focus on mental and physical fitness, disease prevention, healing and rehabilitation, and therapy. Often related to counseling, healing therapies, diet/exercise disciplines.
	Quality of Life	Focus on social well being. Often related to crime prevention, safety, immigration, environment; conflict intervention, advocacy against violence, and peace.
	Human Potential	Focus on personal/vocational fulfillment, education, and human rights. Often includes schools, training, career counseling, and intervention against discrimination.
	Interpersonal Relationships	Focus on family life, marriage, sexuality, and healthy friendships. Often includes marriage counseling and enrichment, divorce counseling, parenting counseling and training, and advocacy for nontraditional relationships.
	Human Destiny	Focus on repentance/forgiveness, conversion, stewardship, and alignment with God's purposes. Often includes revivals, witnessing, canvassing, Bible distribution, prayer chains.

45

Facility Preference for one option over another	Ecclesiastical	The facility must "look like a church": structures traditionally associated with churches: arches and apses, steeples, colored glass windows; linear seating, etc.
	Utilitarian	The facility must be "user-friendly": structures resemble and function like public buildings, entertainment centers, or schools; versatile and flexible.
Symbols Preference for one option over another	Christendom	Signs and architecture use historic symbols associated with Christianity. Symbols supplement classic preaching and teaching.
	Contemporary	Signs and architecture favor symbols and images of broader spiritual significance, which are immediately recognizable by non-Christians.
Technology Preference for one option over another	Modern	Technology primarily enhances print and oral communication. Audio and acoustical improvements; options for reading or listening; sight lines accessibility for seniors.
	Postmodern	Technology primarily enhances multi-sensory interaction. Surround-sound, image, and video improvements; Internet and social media; and multitasking.
Stewardship Preference for one option over another	Unified Budgets	Contribute money to a single general fund, and trust central administrators disburse funds for personnel, program, and institutional overhead. Stability first.
	Designated Giving	Contribute money to personal preferences, and administrators disburse money according to the giver's priorities. Effectiveness first.
Financial Management Preference for one option over another	Informed Philanthropy	Stewardship primarily a financial commitment. They prefer to make informed, independent, confidential commitments for a tax benefit.
	Lifestyle Coaching	Stewardship primarily a lifestyle. They prefer to receive individual counseling; follow models of generosity; expect life benefits in return for obedience.

Communi-cation Alternatives Multiple preferences are possible	Newsprint	Receive knowledge through newspapers, magazines, periodicals; share information through newsletters, mailings; respond to visual advertising.
	Radio	Receive knowledge through AM or FM broadcasts, at home or in vehicles, and often the radio is constantly in the background at home, work, and play.
	Television	Receive knowledge through television programs and commercials, and often the television is constantly on. Images attract attention and stir emotion.
	Telephone	Share information and ideas through oral communication on corded or wireless telephone. Personal conversation, telemarketing, always talking.
	Internet	Receive knowledge by surfing the web, browsing websites, blogs, social networks, and respond well to pop-up advertising. E-mail and text.
	Gatherings	Share information by "hanging out" with others in their affinity group at unique gathering spots; board advertising, free stuff and free promotions.
	Multi-Sources	Communicate in all of the above ways; often simultaneously, using enhanced digital and wireless technology; text across the room or en route.

Church leaders can create their own table that compares lifestyle preferences for ministry in a single template. This can be used as a compact visual guide for reflection and discussion. List the top lifestyle segments in a row, with percentage representation in order of size. Then highlight the boxes for easy comparison, and note the patterns of expectations.

For example, the leaders of St. Anonymous Church plotted their membership using People Plot and printed a Comparative Report. Although 50–70 percent lifestyle representation generally shapes the culture of the community or church, they tracked 76 percent representation in the community and 100 percent of the membership (109,938 and 77 households respectively).

By studying the "Index" column on the right, leaders immediately recognized the imbalance between community and congregational representation. Remember that "100" means the percentage representation is the same. Lower numbers reveal that lifestyle representation is *lower* in the church than in the community; higher numbers reveal that lifestyle representations are *higher* in the church than in the community.

Here is an example of the summary of lifestyle segment profiles for community and congregation. The template is based on the ComparativeInsite Report.

Code	Lifestyle Segment	Study Area		Congregation		Index
		# of Households	% of Community	# of Households	% of Congregation	
L42	Rooted Flower Power	19,109	13.4 percent	16	20.8 percent	155
O51-55	Singles and Starters	31,953	22.3 percent	3	3.9 percent	17
K40, 37	Significant Singles	12,810	9.0 percent	9	11.7 percent	115
C11, C13	Booming with Confidence	12,699	8.9 percent	13	16.9 percent	166
J34	Aging in Place	6,926	4.8 percent	6	7.8 percent	163
E20	No Place Like Home	5,920	4.1 percent	6	15.6 percent	190
Q64, 62, 65	Golden Year Guardians	12,105	7.6 percent	18	15.6 percent	199
B09	Family Fun-tastic	3,323	2.3 percent	5	6.5 percent	283
R66	Dare to Dream	5,093	3.6 percent	1	1.3 percent	36
	Total	109,938	76.0 percent	77	100 percent	

Church leaders developed a table to look specifically at hospitality expectations in the community compared to expectations in the congregation. The table below lists lifestyle segments from highest to lowest, left to right. The top 50 plus percentage of representation is shaded.

Hospi-tality Options	Community Profile							
Code	L42	O51-55	K37-40	C11-13	J34	E20	Q62-65	B09
Percent	13.4 percent	22.3 percent	9.0 percent	8.9 percent	4.8 percent	4.1 percent	7.6 percent	2.3 percent
The Basics							x	x
Multiple Choices	x	x	x	x	x	x	x	x
Healthy Choice	x		x	x	x			
Take Out		x						

The table below lists lifestyle segments represented in the church, from highest to lowest, left to right. Again, the top 50 plus percentage of representation is shaded. Strategic thinkers in the church immediately saw that only one majority lifestyle segment in the community was also represented in the church (L42 "Rooted Flower Power"). This church culture is primarily shaped by lifestyle segments that are much smaller in the community.

Hospi-tality Options	Congregational Profile							
Code	L42	C11-3	E20	Q62-5	K37-0	J34	B09	O51-55
Percent	20.8 percent	16.9 percent	15.6 percent	15.6 percent	11.7 percent	7.8 percent	6.05 percent	6.5 percent
The Basics				x			x	
Multiple Choices	x	x	x	x	x	x	x	x
Healthy Choices	x	x			x	x		
Take Out								x

The community has a clear preference for a blend of "Multiple Choice" and "Healthy Choice" hospitality. This means more than an opulent variety of refreshments following worship. This means people in the community prefer greeters to be trained to be sensitive to community diversity, and held accountable to model positive core values. They would also look for a welcome center in the hub of the church building and a nursery safely located away from exits and close to the sanctuary.

These expectations starkly contrasted with the current hospitality ministry of the church. In fact, postworship refreshments only offered the basics in mediocre coffee, tea, and packaged cookies. Greeters were untrained, and the ministry was assigned to patriarchs and matriarchs of the church who were skeptical of young adults with tattoos and annoyed by precocious children. Instead of a welcome center, there was a memorial wall. Of course, this went against the grain of even the majority of church members, but the board was dominated by Q62–65 "Golden Year Guardians," and they preferred "The Basics." Strategic thinkers in the church now knew how to adjust hospitality to encourage members to linger and visitors to return more than once.

Hospitality is related to outreach, so St. Anonymous church leaders also wanted to improve the relevancy of their outreach ministries. Let's look at the same contrasting lifestyle segments represented in the community and church in the ministry category for outreach. Note that the ministry people like to *receive* (marked with an X) may be different from the ministry they like to *share* (marked with an O).

The strategic thinkers of St. Anonymous decided to *reverse the order* of investigation. Instead of assessing community expectations first, they decided to assess church programs first.

Outreach Options	Congregational Profile							
Code	L42	C11–3	E20	Q62–65	K37–0	J34	B09	O51–55
Percent	20.8 percent	16.9 percent	15.6 percent	15.6 percent	11.7 percent	7.8 percent	6.5 percent	3.9 percent
Survival	o		o	o		o		
Recovery								
Health	x/o	x	x	x			o	
Quality of Life	x/o	o	x	o	o	x/o	o	0
Human Potential		o			x/o		x	x/o
Interpersonal Relationships		x	x		x	x		x/o
Human Destiny				o			x/o	

The profile for the congregation revealed that church members generally preferred to receive ministries related to health (parish nursing, wellness, special support groups, etc.) and quality of life (home safety, emergency services, visitation, etc.) They like to volunteer and share ministries related to survival and quality of life (particularly for children). This was confirmed by observing the outreach ministries already in place.

The strongest outreach programs that receive the most funding and support from the church were related to survival. These included depot ministries for food and clothing, homeless shelters, and day care. These were also priorities for the denomination. However, the church struggled to find volunteers to work in these programs, so that many could only operate as ecumenical sponsorships that tapped a larger pool of volunteers. Fellowship groups were also strong in the church, primarily organized around gender (men's and women's groups) or age (seniors and youth groups).

The profile for the community, however, revealed somewhat different priorities among the largest lifestyle segments represented. This was especially true for the O50 younger lifestyle group of "Singles and Starters" who were significantly underrepresented in the church, even though church members often lamented their inability to attract twenty and thirty-somethings. Note in particular that the table below reveals community priorities for programs related to human potential in addition to quality of life.

This meant that the majority of people in the community were looking for ministries like crime prevention, home security, environmental improvements, or tutoring for children and career counseling for adults; or opportunities to socialize, date, and enjoy life. The boomers in the community also were interested in health programs (like physical fitness, yoga, etc.).

Outreach Options	Community Profile							
Code	L42	O51–55	K37–40	C11–13	J34	E20	Q62–65	B09
Percent	13.4 percent	22.3 percent	9.0 percent	8.9 percent	4.8 percent	4.1 percent	7.6 percent	2.3 percent
Survival	o				o	o	o	
Recovery								
Health	x/o			x		o	x	o
Quality of Life	x/o	o	o	o	x/o	x	o	o
Human Potential		x/o	x/o	o				x
Interpersonal Relationships		x/o	x	x	x	x		
Human Destiny							o	x/o

Strategic thinkers in the church were especially interested to observe those areas of outreach where the desire to *receive* ministry intersected with the urgency to *share* ministry. Programs in these areas would not only bless the community but build relationships between church volunteers and community lifestyles that might increase church participation.

Of course, strategic thinkers in St. Anonymous realized that shifting outreach priorities from survival to human potential might be atypical for the priorities of the denominational culture. And shifting interpersonal relationship ministries away from large gender- and age-based groups toward small affinity-based group might raise the stress level of the "Golden Year Guardians" and "Aging in Place" seniors. That "cost of discipleship" will be considered later.

This comparison of ministry expectations between community and church is one of the most important tasks the board needs to complete in preparation for the leadership summit. It takes time to study and reflect on its significance in each category of ministry. Summit participants should have it available to them two to four weeks in advance.

The *Mission Impact Guide* provides detailed explanations of each of these categories and the alternative choice within each one. My book *See, Know, and Serve* also provides more generic descriptions of each choice. Also, *Worship Ways* describes in detail the different kinds of mission-targeted worship along with specific tactics for implementation. Finally, *Spiritual Leadership* describes in detail the choices for ordered and lay leadership for different lifestyle segments.

Comparative Demographic Data

A great amount of demographic information can be discovered using MissionInsite. Leaders will want to explore the wealth of information in greater detail every five years or so. However, for routine annual planning, the ComparativeInsite Report contains the key information that is vital to strategic planning. Some information is particularly useful for designing worship and planning Christian education:

- average age of head of household
- households with children (with two parents or single parent)
- the age of children in the household
- households without children

Some information is particularly useful for the content and method of preaching and liturgical practices. It can help you know how much they can assume about educational attainment, professional or liberal arts backgrounds.

- level of education (high school or less, college education or professional certification, bachelor or business degrees, and graduate degrees)

- occupations (professional, technical, sales and service, blue collar and white collar, retired)

- other information particularly useful for hospitality, languages, small group affinities, and outreach

- ethnicity for the major groupings of Caucasian and African American, but also nuanced by the countries of origin for Asian and Hispanic publics

- lifestyle segment that further helps you explore expectations for clergy credibility among different cultures and microcultures

Finally, information about estimated household income is particularly useful to understand how, and how much, different people give money to the church.

- Household income can be tracked across twelve different income brackets.

- Estimates for the median household income for each and every lifestyle segment helps you to have a realistic understanding of the financial potential in both the community and the church.

The information provided in a single ComparativeInsite Report can be further explored and nuanced using the "Build a Report" function of MissionInsite. There may be special questions that the board would like to answer before endorsing a creative idea or terminating an apparently ineffective tactic.

Build a Report

An enormous amount of data is available in www.MissionInsite.com. The data provides both detail and trends, and can be provided in tables and charts that can easily be transferred into handouts and visual aids for projection. Here are the basic search areas available to you:

Overview	Demographic Trends Racial Ethnic Trends Population/Households Forecast Summary: Language Spoken at Home Summary: Phase of Life Summary: Population by Household Type Summary: Families in Poverty Summary: Housing Units Mosaic Segments and Mosaic Groups
People	Population Trends (Including Seasonal & Transient) Population Detail (Including Education, Age, Gender, Marital Status, Household Type, Schooling, Spending Patterns) Outreach Opportunities (Including Preschool, Children, Youth & Young Adult)
Households	Income (Including Ethnicity and Forecasts) Type (Single or Family), Size, Poverty and Wealth Vehicle Ownership
Families	Income and Size Forecast With and Without Children Poverty Detail
Diversity	Racial and Ethnic Trends Asian, Hispanic, and Latino Ancestry Language
Housing	Units by Occupancy and Occupancy Type Trends for Dwelling Type and Value Trends for Ownership or Rentals Units by Year Built Mortgage Risk
Work	Employment by Industry Employment Status, Blue and White Collar, by Occupation Unemployment Work (Including Transportation and Travel Time, Home or Away)

The challenge is to sift the wheat from the chaff. As much as 95 percent of the data available is not useful at any given time, but the remaining 5 percent can be critical to the success or failure of a church to adapt programs to be relevant to the mission field.

For example, a common budget and leadership dilemma for churches is whether to continue investing in day-care programs. In many contexts, the trends are revealing. Families with preschool children may be declining, while families with children in elementary and middle school education may be growing. And that may suggest that the church reinvest resources in after-school care and tutoring programs.

Another common example involves urbanization and the transformation of small towns. Established churches struggle with the relevance of worship and membership. They assume that the community norm is still families with children, living in detached homes, with an average residency of five or more years. Therefore, they continue to emphasize children's stories in worship and extended membership training courses. Yet the reality of urbanization is often a new norm for cohabitating young singles without children, living in high-density apartments and townhouses, with an average residency of less than a year. Church programming may well eliminate the children's story and add more music, and reduce membership training timelines and multiply short-term small groups.

Opportunity Scan

It's helpful to know which lifestyle segments are the largest and most influential in your primary mission field. And it's helpful to know what the demographic realities and trends are in your region. But it's even *more* helpful to know exactly *where* the lifestyle segments are most likely to live or exactly *where* these trends are most likely to occur. The next step is to explore population density.

Opportunity Scan allows you to create a color-coded map (and accumulate related statistics) based on population density. The darker blue color reveals the highest population density. Since this is created using the street view, you can see exactly what neighborhoods are involved. You can see which streets or geographical features form the boundaries for that area, and you can get a pretty good idea of the flow or the future for whatever lifestyle or demographic variable you are tracking. Moreover, you can edit the values for population density to narrow or broaden your search.

When you select Opportunity Scan the same menu appears that you saw in Build a Report. This time, however, you select one single variable. Refer to the two previous examples.

Let's suppose a church discovers clear demographic trends that indicate a plateau or decline in families with infants or preschool children at home, and an increase in families or single parents with children in elementary or middle school. They know that they need to shift their ministry and budget from day care to after-school care and tutoring. But *where* will they locate the outreach ministry—and *where* will they advertise it? In this case, Opportunity Scan reveals that they need to acquire rental space several blocks away from the church to locate the outreach site in the most central and accessible spot for commuting parents. They were able to download mailing lists for the exact streets and neighborhoods with the highest population density of households that would likely need this ministry.

Similarly, let's suppose a small-town church is adapting their current worship service or starting a new worship service to be relevant to younger, single or cohabitating, dual-career, childless households that are moving into new apartments and townhouses on the edge of town. Opportunity Scan helps them not only design the worship service but locate and advertise the worship service. In this case, the church realizes that their current location and facility can't be adapted and that they need to locate the worship option to a rented space such as a coffee house or pub on Sunday night. Now they know where to look for the opportunity and exactly where to advertise the new service.

Search Google Maps

Strategic thinkers can further filter their options to save them time and trouble. MissionInsite allows users to link with Google Search to identify exactly where specific public services or businesses are located.

For example, the urban church above can quickly discover where every school is located and where there might be empty retail space to convert into a tutoring center. And the small-town church can quickly discover where every coffee house or pub is located to determine the prime locations. They can even use Google Street Views to actually *see* the property, the related intersections and traffic patterns, and general context.

Once you have specific locations in mind, you can now measure distances between schools and sites, or between church and coffee house, or between any location and another location. Among other things, this can help a leader test whether or not it is reasonable to expect visitors to come or volunteers to commit to the ministry.

Backgrounds

There are different views for your research. On the "Map Tools" menu, select the tab for "Backgrounds." Each view helps you nuance your research in special ways. So far, I've assumed that you are using the "Street View." This is the most common view because it identifies actual routes and street names, defines neighborhoods, and provides direction to access any given site. But there are other views.

- Satellite view provides actual images of the area. These static pictures are taken from satellites and updated regularly. You can increase the magnification to literally see vehicles parked in the church lot and equipment stored in the backyard. You can get a bird's eye view of actual transportation alternatives, living and recreational options, and retail and industrial realities. This view is particularly useful in urban environments to study transportation options or the appearance and proximity of structures, parks, and other sites. This view can be equally helpful in small town or rural environments to see road conditions or the appearance and distance between sites.

- Terrain view offers a three-dimensional topographical map of the region. You can see elevations and benchmarks, understand why roads go this way or that, up or down, and get a sense of the time it takes to travel seemingly short distances. This can be helpful when doing macro regional planning, but it can also be helpful doing micro urban planning. A primary mission field makes better sense when it recognizes significant geographical features that limit population growth or block and guide transportation patterns.

The Hybrid view provides only major routes and the names of population centers against a satellite background. The Basic view only provides routes and place names.

Standard and Customized Layers

The final step in research is to add or remove different layers of civil or ecclesiastical boundaries and markers. The standard boundaries that are available to all users delineate state and county boundaries and labels; zip codes and the names of all towns and cities; census tracts and census blockgroups; and elementary and high school and other districts.

Which layer you use depends on what your research focus is. Consider the two examples we've been following. The urban church that is focused on lifestyle representation for families with elementary and high school age children might be very interested in school districts and zip codes. The small-town church overcome by urbanization, and focused on a growing population density of singles and childless couples, might be very interested in census tracts and blockgroups. Meanwhile, regional leaders thinking about church planting or multisite ministries may want to pay close attention to state and county lines.

The ecclesiastical boundaries are identified in the Map Tools menu as "My Layers." You can overlay on your research church judicatory boundaries and districts (e.g., conferences, synods, diocese, presbyteries). You can also identify the churches of your own denomination.

Again, which layer you use depends on the purpose of your research. Regional church bodies can use this feature to reality test ecclesiastical boundaries that may be out of date and unrealistic. They can also see the proximity of church facilities to each other. The urban church in our example might use this feature to identify potential church partners for collaborative ministries to families with school aged children. The small-town church might use this feature to decide whether to extend the reach of its current site or to create a new and distinct site of worship.

These twelve steps describe the typical flow of demographic and lifestyle research. Of course, the purpose of worship may alter the flow of research in different ways. And there are more advanced techniques that we will explore later. If a board or ministry team masters these twelve techniques, however, they will find it easier to understand their primary mission field, and they will feel more confident to set strategic priorities.

Reality Testing Demographic and Lifestyle Research

Someone will inevitably ask the hard question: Is it true? Is the research accurate at this time in our context or within our own membership?

One reason these questions are asked is that many long-time church members, with long residencies in their communities, have become desensitized to the change and growth around them. Church people in particular bond with an inner circle of friends, a continuous thread of homogeneity that extends over time. They don't really "see" what is happening around them, or they only perceive change when it is threatening.

Meanwhile, other people ask these questions because diversity has accelerated beyond their powers of discernment. People tend to hold on to assumptions, generalizations, and prejudices even though they are no longer useful. They assume "youth" or "seniors," "men" or "women," or people of this ethnicity—or that all cohorts behave the same way and share the same ministry preferences. In fact there are many different kinds of youth and seniors today, many different behavior patterns among men and women. Some of these subgroups work well together and some don't. At the time this book is published, at least ten distinct lifestyle segments include high proportions of African Americans, and twelve distinct segments include high proportions of Hispanic and Latinos. And they don't all share the same ministry preferences.

Strategic thinkers don't assume that their research is correct. Culture and populations are changing so rapidly in many urban and exurban contexts that even the most frequently updated demographic information may still miss important nuances about lifestyle segments in their midst. Some of the methods we once used to test our research are no longer useful. We used to do surveys by mail, e-mail, or door to door, but today many people resent intrusions by "marketers" or are simply not home. We used to do exit surveys among church visitors, but today visitors are more likely to reflect cultural homogeneity than heterogeneity, and their comments distort reality. In fact, with the skepticism and cynicism that pervades the current environment, people are more likely to lie (or distort the truth) in order to camouflage their real reasons for connecting or disconnecting with the church.

One good way to test demographic data is with interview teams. Churches equip a team of two people to make an appointment with some community or business leaders who are in a position to observe trends or compare publics. The teams are equipped with demographic and lifestyle information from their research; share it with key leaders; and listen to feedback that confirms or corrects, nuances and elaborates, the information. Obviously, productive interviews can include social service, health care, emergency and police services, professionals, and municipal planners. Perhaps less obviously, churches can test perceptions about community trends with business leaders. Retail developers, automobile and appliance dealers, and real estate agents are often in excellent positions to notice benchmarks and trends in a community.

A good way to test lifestyle data is with focus groups. A focus group is not just a gathering of friends or miscellaneous people with opinions. Focus groups selectively invite people who belong to a particular lifestyle segment to talk with a team from the church. The invitation is usually extended to neighbors, work associates, or acquaintances of members. They may be invited to lunch or dinner. They are assured that the church will not seek to convert them, pressure them to join, or ask for money. Focus groups are designed in clusters of at least three, and each group is asked the same questions in order to compare group responses. One team member leads the conversation, and the other takes notes.

Spiritual Discernment

The board of a church is different from the board of a nonprofit entity because they also function as spiritual leaders of the congregation. An essential part of long-range strategic thinking is the ability to align all programs, staff, and volunteer teams with the overarching vision and mission that God reveals to the church. This is more challenging than it seems.

First, the church is always in danger of becoming sidetracked. Some aspect of the life and work of the church may be deflected from its purpose or wander from its alignment to God's vision. This might be intentional on the part of controllers in the congregation who consciously try to shape the church around their personal agendas and ambitions. Usually, though, deflection is unintentional but just as dangerous. Without realizing it, leaders and ministry teams may drift from alignment to vision as they encounter other forces at work in culture. The deviation may be subtle at first and become more severe if it goes unchecked. The board finds it more and more difficult to steer in the right direction.

It is often helpful for a board to reflect on corporate addiction. This manifests in self-destructive habits that an organization gradually develops but chronically denies. For example, the church *thinks* it is friendly and at one time was well known for being friendly, but it has gradually turned inward and become more concerned with membership privileges than mission impact on the community. The church is no longer as friendly as it thinks it is. Almost any healthy church behavior can become an unhealthy addiction. A church can become dangerously obsessed about any practice or program, object or individual. The more a church succeeds, the more it avoids risk, because it has more to lose. The fear of loss influences church programming more than the courage to be relevant.

The second great challenge to the spiritual discernment of the board is that God's vision is itself fluid and evolving. There are dimensions to God's vision for the church that have yet to be revealed. The community is constantly changing, and the Spirit is always working in new ways for new situations. The goals to simultaneously multiply disciples and bless the world remain the same, but the strategies are constantly shifting. When it comes to strategic thinking, a good motto is: *All that matters is the gospel. Everything else is just tactics.*

The basic assumption of spiritual discernment for strategic thinking is that church growth and community development are two sides of the same coin. Churches will not grow unless the communities surrounding the church develop socially in healthy ways, and community will not develop and sustain healthy environments unless mature faith and deep spirituality are part of community life. Witness and work, evangelism and social action, faith and life, spirituality and society—are all mutually supportive.

Therefore, spiritual discernment by the board must be more than just prayer and Bible study on the one hand and demographic research on the other. Lifestyle segment analysis has already provided spiritual insight into the varied ways different people quest for God, but it often raises as many questions as it provides answers.

MissionInsite offers psychographic research that reveals even more detail about attitudes and inclinations, social values and religious sensibilities, and the hidden anxieties that drive the quest for God. There are two resources.

Quadrennium Report

A four-year overview of local trending beliefs is also among the "Pre-Defined Reports" of MissionInsite (although individual categories can also be explored separately). This report compares American religious preferences, practices, and beliefs to a particular search area. The report also provides significant indicators about important regional social priorities and attitudes. Again, these are presented as a range between extremes of importance *compared to national average*. The board can compare the depth of faith, commitment to religion, agreement or disagreement with various ethical viewpoints, and other local priorities to what is normative in America.

- beliefs about God
- beliefs about Jesus
- beliefs about social and moral issues
- presence of "nones" (i.e., no religious preference or no faith at all)
- changing trends in Christian religious preference
- changing trends from Christian to non-Christian preferences
- current significance of religious faith to daily living
- changing trends in the significance of religious faith to daily living

- life concerns

- media preference

The board can discern how traditional or nontraditional community views on religion are and ponder how this might impact (for example) liturgical practices or public policies of the church. The board can track both religious membership and relevance of faith and ponder (for example) how their penetration rate in the community is changing and what they might do about it. The board can identify key concerns in the community and ponder (for example) how this influences the topics of preaching and the affinities of small groups. And finally, the board can understand media preference and ponder (for example) how this influences technology upgrades and advertising.

Worldviews

The board can also use the "Build a Report" function of Mission-Insite to track specific attitudes, perspectives, priorities, and concerns in the community. Each specific item can be compared to a list of priorities. More importantly, each item can be mapped geographically and color coded for population density using the Opportunity Scan tool.

- life concerns and well being

- lifestyle preferences

- personal perspectives

- charitable contributions

- religious practices

- social values

The board can perform an Opportunity Scan on any item to see the highest population density of people with that attitude, perspective, priority, or concern. That, in turn, can not only help them reprioritize outreach programs but also learn exactly where to locate or promote a particular outreach program.

Worldviews in any given search area are compared with the state average. The people in any given search area are well above average, somewhat above average, average, somewhat below average, or well below average. Leaders are most interested in ways that the people in their primary mission field are well above, or well below, state average.

Some worldviews provide insights that can be readily used to adapt and target ministries. The Opportunity Scan tool can isolate a particular "Life Concern." For example, you can see population density for people who feel very lonely in the world, people who worry all the time, and people with other emotional or relational concerns. Churches can quickly learn where to place a small group or outreach ministry, and develop mailing lists to advertise opportunities for building healthy and safe interrelationships.

Other worldviews provide interesting insights, but these require more prayerful reflection to interpret their meaning for Christian ministries. The Opportunity Scan tool can reveal preferences, perspectives, and social values. For example, churches might ponder why the population in their mission field includes well above state average "women who hate housework" or well below average "parents who are indulgent toward children." Such information might lead a church to develop a small affinity group for career women who struggle to balance work and family responsibilities, or help a church structure their day-care program or Sunday school. But more profoundly, it can suggest deeper insights into relative desire for absolutes and dogmas versus openness to ambiguity and spiritual journeys.

Reality Testing

Churches tend to overprogram and underspiritualize their strategic thinking. In other words, they take far too much time researching information, surveying opinions, reading books, and reviewing denominational precedents. They spend very little energy in deep prayer, listening to the public, reflecting on scripture, experiencing the real presence of Christ, and meditating on the identity and purpose of the church. Strategic thinking corrects that mistake.

At the same time leaders are researching the primary mission field, the congregation as a whole should be engaged in the thought process. The following exercises are designed to involve as many people as possible. The purpose is to raise awareness of the trust and purpose of the church, immerse members in the mission field, and stimulate discussion about the future direction of outreach. The feedback can be collated and forwarded to leaders in preparation for the leadership summit.

Prayer Walks

Prayer walking combines personal immersion in the mission field with a simple journaling process. Choose any neighborhood within the primary mission field. This may be a new subdivision, a neighborhood in cultural or economic transition, or particularly busy street, but encourage people to choose an area within the mission field that they *don't usually frequent.*

The prayer walk group is self-selected and usually not more than 3–6 people. These friends (singles, couples, or families) invest 2–3 hours during the week to walk. You may wish to take notes or record verbal comments into a handheld device. You may want to stop for coffee and conversation within the group or with perfect strangers, but avoid focusing on yourselves and your friends. Pay attention to others.

- Observe: Look carefully at people, noting their age, culture, affluence or poverty, conversation and behavior. Note signs, advertising, architecture, technologies, and other things that reveal the nature and mission of the place in which people move.

- Imagine: Observe people again, and imagine whether they are married or single, what occupations they might have, and what life issues and key questions are on their minds. Speculate why people choose to be *here*, rather than someplace else.

- Pray: Look for signs that the Holy Spirit is here, at this place, and among these people. Pray for strangers, and name the gift of grace you hope God will give the people in this location.

After the prayer walk, gather in a place that is both public (where you can see the diversity of the community) and quiet (where you can talk comfortably and confidentially). Answer the following questions.

What Is the Agony That I See?

One can substitute words such as *yearning, issues, concerns,* and perceived *questions.* I prefer to use the word *agony* to emphasize that prayer walkers are trying to discern the deeper anxieties and desperate urgency that surface unexpectedly in the behavior, language, art, and habits of people in a particular demographic or lifestyle segment.

What Is the Blessing I Long to Give?

One can substitute words such as *social service, message, encouragement,* and *donation.* I prefer to use the word *blessing* to maximize imagination and deliberately connect our giving to God's grace. *Blessing* connotes both outward help and inner renewal.

What Is the Image of Hope?

Prayer walkers are surrounded by an experience of life, and their two or three hours of walking are like a snapshot from a larger motion picture that preceded their arrival and will continue when they leave. How would that snapshot change if God worked a miracle? If the *agony* of the people and the *blessing* of God intersected, what would that scene look like?

The image of hope may connect with the vision of the church—or it may disconnect with the vision of the church. Either way, this gives strategic thinkers food for thought. It is often helpful to conclude the reflection during the prayer walk by answering the question, *If I could rename my church to capture the attention of "strangers to grace," what would it be?*

Prayer walkers can send their completed journals or key insights to the church office where they can be collated (without naming the authors). Preachers and worship leaders may share selected insights with the congregation and with the leaders who will eventually participate in the summit.

These insights shape the prayers of the people and provoke conversations among small groups.

Listening Triads

Listening triads are groups of three people who simply observe together. Make a list of many places people in the primary mission field are apt to gather: shopping malls, sports arenas, restaurants and coffee shops, bars, theaters, big box stores, and so on. The goal is to be stationary and invisible, observing people interact with each other and their surroundings in a public place. The triad is particularly useful for officers, staff, board members, and key lay leaders of the church. Three people are a small enough number to blend into a public place, but a large enough number to see things from different perspectives.

The covenant of a triad can be very flexible. Typically, they follow this exercise over several weeks. Each week they meet at one participant's home to prepare themselves. They review the commentaries on the ministry expectations of lifestyle segments found in *Mission Impact*, often concentrating on lifestyle segments currently non- or under-represented in the congregation. They may read a portion of scripture specifically related to the apostolic "Gentile Mission" and then pray for the guidance of the Holy Spirit.

They then proceed to the gathering spot of choice. (If the location is a store, it is sometimes wise to make your purpose known to security!) Taking notes is usually intrusive, and conversation often sidetracks attention. Observe, listen, and remember naturally, without invading privacy.

- Notice the spontaneous behavior patterns of different groups of people, because these often reveal the positive and negative core values that they reenact at work, home, and play.

- Notice the appearance of individuals (clothing, jewelry and accessories, body art, etc.). These often provide clues to their spirituality, religious convictions, or superstitions.

- Notice how people socialize. Watch what they eat and how they eat, how long they linger and how fast they walk, and other socialization patterns that provide clues for what each lifestyle segment considers relevant or radical hospitality.

- Notice the advertising and signage that surrounds people. Marketers are very sensitive to lifestyles, and the form and media, content and images reveal much about how people communicate and learn.

The exercise of listening might last one to two hours, each week in a different context. At the end, triad members assemble again in a quiet place or perhaps return to a participant's home. There they debrief and pray aloud for strangers.

These experiences often stir the heart and move people to tears. Since the act of listening is passive and triads don't intervene to say or do anything, their active response is prayer. They should share their feelings and observations with the pastor and designers of worship. Their insights can then shape the prayers of the people, selection of hymns and songs, projected images, and other aspects of worship on Sunday morning.

Community research and spiritual discernment allow the board and pastor (or senior staff) to compare and contrast the relevance of ministries to the current membership with the need for relevance in the community. They can clearly see how the church effectively blesses some lifestyle segments, but needs to make changes or create options of ministry to effectively bless lifestyle segments in the community that are underrepresented in the church.

Chapter 4

The Way of Strategic Thinking: The Path of Ministry Teams

At the same time that the board is doing research, ministry team leaders are assessing the faithfulness and effectiveness of church programs and church leaders. Eventually the insights from both groups will be merged to set priorities for the coming year(s).

Understand the different roles of board and team leaders in the process. Most churches either fail to divide the labor of strategic thinking or they burden the paid staff with doing it all. The result is that research is inaccurate and assessment is inadequate. When that happens, the church is unable to set priorities, and they end up simply repeating the same programs, with the same handful of volunteers, over and over again.

Churches that fail to divide the labor properly usually find that board and staff have got the method backward. Instead of research, the board tries to micromanage programs. Instead of assessment, the staff is projecting personal tastes and priorities onto the lifestyle segments within and beyond the church. Churches that burden staff with doing everything tend to concentrate on demographic research but not spiritual discernment. As a result, church programs become less and less aligned to congregational vision and are driven by other ideological or theological agendas.

The one person who straddles the work of both research and assessment is the pastor or lead minister. She or he works with the board to help guide and interpret research. And she or he delegates authority and responsibility to other paid staff or volunteer ministry team leaders to assess the faithfulness and effectiveness of the various programs or leaders within the sphere of influence of each team.

The Two Principles of Assessment

It is vital to understand the two basic principles with which church leaders should evaluate any program or leader. These two principles are closely tied to the "ends policies" of the church, and to the measureable outcomes defined by leaders the previous year. Literally anything can (and must!) be evaluated using these criteria, from the smallest tactic (e.g., what kind of coffee to serve in postworship refreshments) to the boldest strategy (e.g., what major outreach ministry will we invest the most of our money and energy to implement).

These same two principles will eventually be used to set priorities for the coming year(s). You might say that the measureable outcomes defined at the beginning of a period of ministry become the means of assessment at the end of a period of ministry. Look at it this way. At the end of the year church leaders (board and staff) must ask and answer this question: *How successful were we this year?*

The questions cannot be avoided by a vague assumption that all that matters is that we try hard and enjoy the journey. Christ clearly expects the church to accomplish something. The answers can't be based on the wishful thinking of leaders; or the tacit assumption that corporate good feelings, charitable intentions, happy pastoral relations, and a balanced budget suffice for the advancement of the realm of God.

When churches do not evaluate success, they just preserve the status quo. Their focus is internal and their obsession is with harmony. The church does not grow and becomes increasingly irrelevant to the mission field. Since demographic and lifestyle research is all about focusing the *heartburst* for mission, it becomes clear that the heart of the church only bursts for themselves.

In recent years, a false dichotomy between church growth and social action has needlessly divided the church. Some leaders and members want to grow the organization; other leaders and members want to bless the community. In fact, both are right. The church cannot sustain and expand social service unless it grows as an organization, and the organization cannot grow unless it is relevant and beneficial to the surrounding community.

The *Principle of Acceleration* is the first key criterion for assessment. I sometimes call it the "Principle of Zoom." Every program and leader of the church should effectively grow the church. This may mean numerical or financial growth, or relational and spiritual growth. It may mean more worshipers, the multiplication of small groups, or the swell of new volunteers. Acceleration happens when churches exert themselves to learn more, try different things, welcome new people, raise the bar of accountability, increase resources, and generally get bigger and bolder.

The *Principle of Impact* is the second key criterion for assessment. I sometimes call it the "Principle of Punch." Every program or leader of the church should effectively change the world for the better. This may mean personal transformation or social transformation. It may mean incremental social change or dramatic social change. It may be known to a few or known to the entire community. The community will be different because the church existed this year. It may be a little better or a lot better, but it will be better.

Exactly *what* ministry team leaders evaluate to measure acceleration and impact may vary from church to church or context to context. For example, one church might want to evaluate the number of Hispanic/Latino participants in worship (acceleration) and the extent to which the standard of living for Hispanic/Latino immigrants is improving (impact). Another church might want to evaluate the multiplication of midweek small groups (acceleration) and the percentage of congregational members personally volunteering in outreach ministries (impact). *What* is evaluated is clearly related to the measureable outcomes that the church set out to achieve.

Regardless of *what* is measured, the *method of measuring* is basically the same. There are three ways to measure anything.

Statistics

Statistics are the most obvious form of measurement. Quantities and percentages, trends, and other numbers can reveal a great deal about the relative success or failure of a church in acceleration and impact. Consider the first example above. If the church sets out to increase Spanish-speaking participation by 20 percent in a given year but only increases participation by 5 percent, then the church is not accelerating very successfully.

Stories

Counting stories of a certain kind is a way to assess qualitative change that can't be easily quantified. Consider the second example above. It may be difficult to measure the participation of all members, in all kinds of outreach, within and beyond the church, over a given year. However, you can gather mission *stories* as you overhear excited conversations about the joys of service, and print them in your newsletter. If the church sets out to mature members to higher commitment in service, and the Mission Moment in worship suddenly lasts longer than the sermon, the church must be doing something right.

Feedback

Intentionally gathering feedback from other church and social service partners is another way to assess both quantitative and qualitative change. Board and/or ministry team leaders can make appointments with nonprofit CEOs, health care specialists, and other community leaders. If the church sets out to increase the standard of living of immigrants in the community, and social service partners are aware of and enthusiastic for the outreach of the church, then church leaders know that they are successfully impacting the community.

Whether you measure acceleration or impact, you must count something. And as you gather statistics, stories, and feedback, you can begin to develop an overall "score" for the relative success of your church.

Using MissionInsite to Assess Ministry Relevance

Ministry team leaders can follow the same steps of research outlined earlier for the work of the board. In order to assess acceleration and impact, however, they will need to use more advanced features.

People Plot Plus

The board can research the exact location of members, and eventually generate a ComparativeInsite Report that will compare proportionate representation of demographic benchmarks and lifestyle segments. But there is more that you can do with People Plot.

Team leaders can track increases or decreases in different categories. Perhaps the most important is the ability to track and locate first- and second-time visitors to worship. You can see not only who they are but where they come from, and understand which neighborhoods are being impacted the most or least.

Data can also be collected in People Plot regarding congregant status (member by baptism, profession of faith, transfer, etc.) You can measure the impact of evangelism or track the acceleration of church membership. Indeed, MissionInsite allows you to customize data collection for almost any demographic category. For example, you can track increases or decreases in young families with infant or preschool children, empty-nesters, and so on.

An additional feature is available to MissionInsite subscribers called "Donor Center." This helps churches identify and track financial donations to both churches and charities. If a church includes a separately incorporated faith-based nonprofit in its ministry, Donor Center can link to additional resources specifically tailored to nonprofit organizations.

This research is cumulative. It gets more and more helpful as People Plot is updated annually. Ministry teams can chart the growth or decline of different kinds of individuals, families, or lifestyle segments over time to measure acceleration and impact.

Penetration Rate

Take another look at the ComparativeInsite Report generated for your church. At the very least it provides data about the specific area you are researching. The left-hand column tells you the number of congregants and congregant households, population by individuals and households, included in the search area. The right-hand column, however, gives insight into the actual impact of the church on that population.

Compare the total number of lifestyle segments represented in the search area with the total number of lifestyle segments *currently represented in the church.* The difference is often dramatic. I often see churches that include only a a small percentage of the lifestyle segments that actually exist in the primary mission field. Later in the ComparativeInsite Report (as I said earlier) you can identify the specific lifestyle segments that are over- or under-represented in the church. The point is that a healthy church is more heterogeneous than homogeneous and should closely mirror the diversity of the mission field.

The Estimated Household Penetration Rate is also provided. Of course, the larger the search area is, the lower the penetration rate will be. The most useful numbers are gleaned from smaller research areas like a single neighborhood, subdivision, or town. Even then, don't be surprised if the number seems low. In many studies, a penetration rate of just 1.5 percent can represent a significant number of households. The value of this information, however, is cumulative. When you update the data annually, you can chart the relative increase or decrease of congregational impact in any given search area.

Penetration rate can tell you something about both acceleration and impact. The total number of individuals, families, or households gives you insight into church growth; but specific trends regarding particular kinds of individuals, families, or households reveal how effective you are in changing the lives of people in the community.

Financial Potential

The corporate researchers who gather and sort date about lifestyle segments can provide estimated median household incomes for each segment. This information is helpful for nonprofit fundraising, but the information is even more suggestive to churches. After all, financial giving is part of a spiritually disciplined life.

The last pages of the ComparativeInsite Report provide estimated median income for lifestyle segments represented in the congregation. The total amount is often surprising. Even when the total amount (gross income) is corrected for the total household income of church members after taxes (net income) the amount is often still surprising. MissionInsite projects what congregational giving might be based on 2 percent, 3 percent, 5 percent, 7 percent, and 10 percent (tithing) giving. Not only does this give you an objective number for capital fund-raising, but it provides insight into the real spiritual discipline of church members. Are they really putting their money where their mouth is?

The information about financial potential can also provide insight into the vitality of the church as a whole. We know that people are motivated to generosity for three basic reasons. People give to big, bold, faithful visions; credible ordained and lay spiritual leaders; and opportunities to make a real difference in the world. If financial giving is growing, then this suggests the vision is bold enough, the leaders are credible enough, and the community is really blessed. If not, then something about vision, credibility, and outcomes is demotivating the membership.

I find this information is particularly helpful when pastoral leadership changes or when interim ministry is in place. You can literally take a "before" and "after" snapshot of congregational vitality.

The information gleaned from these three advanced features of MissionInsite provides a cumulative big picture of congregational acceleration and impact.

For example, the ministry team leaders of St. Anonymous Church are beginning an assessment of the past year's ministries (i.e., the various programs and activities in which they invest their time, talent, and money).

First, they use the advanced features of People Plot. They have been updating data for five years now and are beginning to follow some important trends. The good news is that membership is growing. However, the data reveals several disturbing trends.

- The number of first- and second-time visitors who never establish an enduring connection with the church is much, much larger than the number of visitors who eventually join the church.

- Membership grows primarily through transfers of membership, and the number of adults who join by a first-time profession of faith has steadily declined over five years.

- Church member households have been growing in every neighborhood in their primary mission field except one. The church has *not* been gaining ground in the largely African American neighborhood just a mile southeast of the church.

- Membership gains have been primarily among young families and seniors, but empty-nest adult households represented in the membership are declining—and this is the group that primarily feeds lay leadership.

Leaders don't leap to any conclusions, but they will communicate these concerns to the team clusters that will be meeting around the subsystems for "traction" and "direction."

Next the leaders of St. Anonymous Church investigated their penetration rate into a number of smaller search areas. Overall, their score was 2.3, which was up from 1.8 just five years ago. However, their lack of presence in the African American neighborhood was confirmed. Moreover, out of thirty-eight lifestyle segments present in their larger primary mission field, the church only included thirteen. That had not changed in five years. Although church members cared for each other very much, the congregation had not made any progress mirroring the mission field. Among the missing lifestyles were several lifestyle segments coded O50-O55, belonging to a group known as "Singles and Starters." These included young singles and cohabitating childless couples just starting careers and living in apartment buildings around the expanding university.

Finally, St. Anonymous leaders printed a new ComparativeInsite Report to study the financial potential of the church as a whole. The good news was that the total combined median incomes of the lifestyle segments currently represented in the church were over $6 million. If church members were to donate just 3 percent of their net incomes, leaders estimated they could sustain a church budget of over $800,000. Unfortunately, their current budget was around $500,000. Church leaders began to wonder if their vision was not big and bold enough, if their staff and board were not sufficiently credible as spiritual leaders, or if their outreach ministries were just not compelling enough to motivate greater generosity.

The big picture of church effectiveness provided much to celebrate but also a number of concerns. However, we know that "the devil is in the details" and the "angels are in the actions" of what is going on day by day.

Basic Systems for Acceleration and Impact

Ministry team leaders, unlike board members, have firsthand experience in the primary mission field. This helps them nuance and interpret the data to evaluate success. Team leaders need to interpret lifestyle segment expectations more closely. This is the real value of Mission Impact. This is a commentary I developed for MissionInsite subscribers based on cluster research by companies like Experian[6] who use digital information to create lifestyle portraits from tracking credit cards or other ways people appear on the grid; plus my own experience more than twenty years as an international consultant; plus the insights and ongoing corrections of consulting and denominational colleagues.

Earlier I summarized the eleven different filters I use to identify for church leaders the leadership and ministry expectations of each lifestyle segment and group. Team leaders delve deeply into this information as

---

6. See www.Experian.com.

they assess the relative effectiveness of the programs in their sphere of influence for acceleration and impact.

The particular method of assessment that will be helpful for ministry teams to use Mission Impact for program and leadership assessment is summarized by the following diagram.

Imagine the church as a vehicle driving down the road. The people on the bus must be universally accountable to a consensus of trust. The right *leadership* (clergy, staff, and board) must drive the bus. The purpose or vision of the church emerges from trust and lights up the path ahead. And the bus must travel in the right direction so that measurable outcomes are directly aligned to mission statement.

The church gets TRACTION on the road to mission as the rear wheels spin around relevant facilities and technologies:

- radical hospitality
- targeted worship
- vital small groups

The church STEERS down the road to mission as the front wheels spin around relevant financial management:

- Christian education
- targeted outreach
- clear communication

The synergy of hospitality, worship and small groups generates energy for mission; and the synergy of education, outreach, and mentoring generates institutional participation. Ministry preferences for lifestyle segments inside and outside the church shape the tactics so that the church can arrive at its mission destination.

The chart below summarizes the key elements that make a church grow and go (another way to describe *acceleration* and *impact*).[7]

---

7. This image originally appeared in my book *Church Mergers: A Guidebook for Missional Change*, with Page Brooks (Lanham, MD: Rowan and Littlefield, 2016).

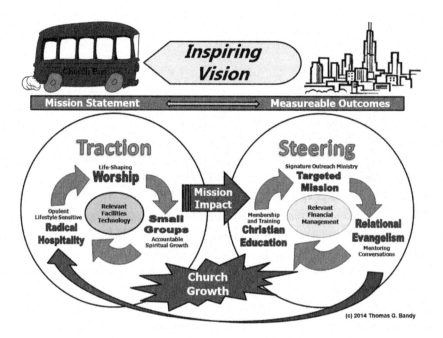

Ministry teams begin assessment by working in clusters related to the key pieces of this diagram. The reason you begin assessment as a cluster is that several teams essentially contribute to a single subsystem of congregational life and mission.

- The first cluster includes teams that contribute most to *traction*: hospitality, worship, and small midweek spiritual growth groups. In smaller churches, teams related to congregational caregiving are also included.

- The second cluster includes teams that contribute most to *steering*: Christian education and membership training, local and global outreach, and evangelism and mentoring. In smaller churches, teams related to resources (property and finance) are also included.

In larger churches, the teams related to caregiving and resources might meet separately as individual clusters.

The number and design of the clusters may vary from church to church due to the tradition or size of the congregation, but the steps of initial assessment are the same.

Review Congregational DNA

Each cluster recalls and celebrates the unique identity of the church. This is revealed though the foundation of trust (i.e., core values and bedrock beliefs) and the motivating vision (i.e., inspiring image or theme song). This essentially describes the positive behavioral expectations of ministry team participants and the clarity of purpose as each team contributes to the overall process of multiplying disciples who bless the world in the name of Christ. Simply stated, each cluster recalls the Heart Beat and the Heart Song that defines identity and purpose.

Review Diverse Lifestyle Expectations

As I explained earlier, the culture of any given community or organization is largely shaped by the top 50–70 percent of the lifestyle segments it includes. It is easy to identify the largest lifestyle segments that comprise this critical mass for both community and congregation using the ComparativeInsite Report.

Each cluster prayerfully and thoughtfully reviews the detailed, and often contrasting, expectations of lifestyle segments for the respective ministries that comprise traction and steering. The teams can now explore in detail the relevance or irrelevance of their programs to the mission field or membership. They can see how they will need to adapt in order to connect with lifestyle segments underrepresented in the church and how they will need to manage the stress of change of lifestyle segments that are overrepresented in the church.

Compare Mission to Measureable Outcomes

Each cluster recalls and celebrates the mission statement of the church, and specifically connects this with the measureable outcomes that will measure success for each ministry team. Usually, each cluster will have before them about ten outcomes (divided among various teams). These outcomes will essentially establish the synergy or flow of ministry in each subsystem.

The assessment of acceleration and impact doesn't just depend on something as abstract as alignment to a mission statement. It also depends on how effectively programs bless a particular public in a special way. I call this *heartburst*. The heartburst of a church may not be for one of the largest lifestyle segments in the community but rather for a smaller lifestyle segment whose social predicament or quest for God touches the heart of the church.

Outcomes should translate into *passions*. True teams don't pursue outcomes for which they are not passionate, and they are never satisfied with passion unless they can measure fulfillment through practical outcomes.

Rate Systemic Effectiveness

Initially, the rating system can be as simple as assessing programs as *strong, struggling,* or *weak* (on a scale of 1–3). This is especially helpful for the cluster to understand the relative contributions of each ministry team to the subsystem itself.

1	*Strong*	reliable, consistent, celebrated
2	*Struggling*	unreliable, only occasionally effective, often stressful
3	*Weak*	rarely successful, consistently ineffective, always stressful

The assessment of systemic effectiveness takes into consideration the relative strength or weakness of a subsystem. The effectiveness of traction or steering is not due to any specific program but to the way each team interconnects with the other teams. The programs in each time feed the next team, and the volunteers from one team may migrate to another team. The overall effectiveness of traction or steering might be summarized in the following chart:

Score	1	2	3
Team Leadership			
Paid Staff			
Volunteers			
High Trust			
Respectful Values			
Credible Convictions			
Clear Purpose			
Powerful Passions			
Measureable Outcomes			
Traction			
Radical Hospitality			
Life-Shaping Worship			
Small Groups			
Sensitive Caregiving			
Steering			
Christian Training			
Targeted Mission			
Relational Evangelism			
Leadership Accountability			
Total Score			

Church leaders can now discern patterns of relative strength or weakness in the key subsystems of congregational life and mission. The total score helps church leaders glimpse the most urgent areas for action. They have a better idea what areas of ministry are working very well, where tweaks and changes can be left up to the individual teams; and what programs are struggling or weak and require closer attention.

Let's continue to use St. Anonymous Church as an example of church assessmen. Specifically, let's follow the "Traction Cluster" of the church. These included two distinct hospitality teams (greeters/ushers and refreshment servers); three distinct worship teams (preachers and liturgists, choir, and praise band); three small group teams (Bible study, affinity groups, and addiction intervention groups); and two caregiving teams (a regular lay visitation team and a special Stephen Ministry team). The synergy of these teams working together would provide traction for the church to move forward.

First, the cluster remembered, pondered, and celebrated the DNA of the church. The foundation of trust among the teams of the cluster seemed sound. The choir and the praise band had overcome petty jealousies years ago and now respected and supported the unique music of each group. They all shared the same practices of accountability, and while everyone relied on mutual honesty, nobody felt judged. Clarity of purpose was a cause for concern. A number of musicians in both the choir and praise band seemed to be passionate about performance but not particularly articulate about mission. They tended to pack up and leave after worship without mingling with members and seekers during refreshments.

Second, the Traction Cluster studied mission impact and spent considerable time reflecting on the needs and yearnings of the lifestyle segments in and beyond the church. They realized that the lifestyle segments overrepresented in the church tended to prefer a slow-paced blend of educational and caregiving worship. One result was that conversation during refreshments following worship tended to be about relatively mundane things like sports, weather, and grandchildren, as people gathered in small and relatively exclusive friendship circles. Another result was that the most successful small groups tended to focus on fellowship or Bible study but did not build very deep intimate friendships nor markedly hone personal spiritual practices.

Meanwhile, they also realized that the lifestyle segments underrepresented in the church generally preferred a fast-paced blend of educational and inspirational worship. That included both the African American segments in the neighborhood to the southeast and the "Singles and Starters" lifestyle group that lived in crowded apartments surrounding the university. If they wanted to reach them, they probably would need to upgrade hospitality with more training and empower musicians to be more articulate about faith.

Third, the Traction Cluster reviewed the measureable outcomes that challenged each of the teams during the previous year. They rejoiced to see that they had achieved or surpassed many of the outcomes expected of them. They now had multiple teams of greeters at every entrance/exit before, during, and after worship; and the preachers were receiving very positive feedback. In addition, three new small groups (all related to fellowship) had emerged in the past year. On the other hand, they had failed to stem the tide of first- and second-time visitors who never ultimately connected with the church; the more contemporary worship service had not grown by more than a few households; and feedback about the friendliness of the church from the participants in the addiction intervention groups was still not very enthusiastic.

Finally, the Traction Cluster began to rate their combined systemic effectiveness. They used a simple method. Everyone completed the form (see above) privately and anonymously; the scores were averaged by each team leader and shared; and then these were again averaged to create a total score. Then they stepped back to look for patterns.

- Paid staff leadership was strong, but the lay volunteer leaders were struggling. Some felt confident and competent, some were confident about their purpose but anxious about their competence, and a few were very confident but unclear about mission.

- Trust was strong. People treated one another, and visitors, with all the values of the fruits of the Spirit; and they were all committed to the bedrock beliefs of the church.

- Purposefulness was usually strong but occasionally struggling. As noted before, some outcomes had not been achieved, leaving team members frustrated. And increasingly it seemed that hospitality and small group leaders were losing their passion to bless strangers to grace.

All in all, the sensitive caregiving ministries seem uniformly strong. The other teams were pretty strong overall but with clear weaknesses in individual programs. Each team would need to address each program one by one to assess acceleration and impact. As a cluster, however, the teams began to understand how the wheels on the bus were sometimes slipping, losing traction. They began to understand why too many visitors were lost, some lifestyle segments were missing, and personal spiritual practices were spotty at best. More importantly, they began to see what they could do to change that.

Assessment Process

The area of ministry or sphere of influence of a ministry team can be defined in many ways. A typical example is based on my previous diagram for traction and steering. The ministry areas may be more detailed if the strategic thinking of the ministry team identifies particular problems for current tactics or new opportunities for innovative ministry. The ministry areas may be identified as follows:

Traction		
Hospitality	Including activities like:	
	Sunday Fellowship:	Greeting, ushering, refreshments
	Special Occasions:	New Year, Easter, Mother's Day, Thanksgiving, Christmas
	Lifecycle Events:	Weddings, funerals, baptisms, communion
	Special Events:	Suppers, catering, etc
Worship	Including activities like:	
	Sunday Worship:	First service, second service, etc.
	Sacramental Events:	Baptisms, communions, confirmations
	Special Worship:	New Year, Easter, Mother's Day, Thanksgiving, Christmas
	Lifecycle Events:	Christenings, weddings & anniversaries, funerals & memorials
Small Groups	Including activities like:	
	Gender Groups:	Women, men
	Age Groups:	Youth, seniors
	Affinity Groups:	Hobby, craft, sports, choirs, bands, etc.
	Support Groups:	Prayer, recovery, special needs
Caregiving	Including activities like:	
	Visitation:	Home, hospital, nursing home, correctional facility
	Intervention:	Acute care, intervention, emergencies
	Counseling:	Marriage, grief, personal and family
	Mentoring:	Vocation, spiritual disciplines
	Mediation:	Conflict

Communi-cation	Including activities like:	
	Print:	Newsletters, handouts, books,
	Audio:	Radio broadcast, recording, telephone networks
	Video:	TV broadcast, taping
	Digital:	Website, e-mail, blog, text
	Personal:	Announcements, speeches
Steering		
Education & Training	Including activities like:	
	Sunday School:	Nursery, preschool, children, youth, adult
	Seasonal Studies:	Advent, Lent, etc.
	Study Groups:	Bible study, gifts discernment, personal discovery,
	Special Events:	Workshops, seminars
	Training	Membership, leadership
Outreach	Including activities like:	
	Local:	Survival, health, recovery, quality of life, human potential, interpersonal relationships, witnessing
	Denominational:	Social service, health care, advocacy
	Global:	Disaster relief, medical mission, famine relieve, etc.
	Partnerships:	Ecumenical, para-church, service agencies
Finance	Including activities like:	
	Fund-Raising:	Budget development, annual stewardship campaigns
	Special Fund-Raising:	Capital campaigns, grant applications
	Bookkeeping:	Investments & debt management
Property & Trusteeship	Including activities like:	
	Facility:	Renovation, maintenance, accessibility, safety, insurance
	Technology:	Audio, video, appliances, utilities
	Landscaping:	Environmental protection, parking, maintenance
	Other Sites:	Management, maintenance

Before assessment can begin, the ministry teams must revisit and identify the measureable outcomes that they set out to accomplish with all of their activities. Initially, this may be difficult to do. The truth is that many churches have not defined measureable outcomes in the past, which makes it more difficult to evaluate success in the future. That pattern will change as you follow this process.

For those who are unfamiliar or uncomfortable with measureable outcomes, let's use the example of St. Anonymous Church once again. Since we only focused on the ministry areas and teams related to *traction* when we rated systemic effectiveness, we will focus on the same area and teams to identify measureable outcomes. (Note how they clearly intend to measure success using all three methods to gather *statistics, stories,* and *feedback.*) Here is their chart:

St. Anonymous Church	
Overall Church Goals	Grow the church to a stable and involved membership in the range of 650–700 members.
	Outstanding pastoral leadership for spiritual growth and administration.
	Enthusiastic, committed, approachable staff & board to focus mission and coordinate service.
	Family feeling of mutual support and shared service.
	Happy and engaged congregation with strong Christian beliefs and values.
Hospitality Outcome	Multiple choices (opportunities and methods) to welcome, build relationships and encourage significant conversations between members and visitors, and move people into further participation in the church.
Worship Outcome	Sunday worship is a perfect blend of inspiration giving hope for the future, and education giving insight into faith and morality. Occasional worship that celebrates important religious and cultural festivals, and gathers large crowds within which mature Christians can network informally with spiritual seekers.
Small Group Outcome	Constantly multiplying Covenant Groups for intentional spiritual growth and deeper interpersonal relationships.
Caregiving Outcome	Excellent, responsive, confidential lay ministry teams trained, coordinated, and accountable to the lead pastor.

In the example of St. Anonymous above, there are essentially four teams that are working together to give the church *traction.* Each ministry team compiles a list of all the programs or activities currently active within their sphere of influence. How detailed that list is, however, may be different from church to church, and even from time to time.

For example, a worship team may include in that list each and every special worship event (Thanksgiving, Christmas, Mother's Day, Easter, Pentecost, etc.); or it may just put them all together in a general category of special worship services through the year. The choice probably depends on the intuition of the leader, or the special request of the pastor or board.

Once the list is compiled into a table, the team reviews each program or activity using the principles of acceleration and impact on a scale of 1–10. A score of 1–3 means that the program is failing badly and needs urgent correction. A score of 4–7 means that the program is doing OK, but not achieving its full potential. A score of 8–10 means that the program is very successful, and whatever tweaks and improvements are necessary can be easily managed by the team.

Ongoing Programs

In a perfect world, everything a church does should be a perfect 10 for both acceleration and impact, but we know that rarely happens. Some things we do will make the church grow but won't change the world much. Other things we do may dramatically change the community for the good but won't bring many new worshipers or members. In the end, every ministry team balances the list of programs to achieve both acceleration and impact, but the composite score should still be relatively high in order to be successful. A combined score of 2–6 means that the program is in such desperate shape that church leaders may wonder why they should spend resources to do it. A combined score of 7–15 means that the program is doing OK, but not achieving its full potential. And a combined score of 15+ means that the program is doing very well already and the ministry team can manage improvements as they go.

Note that the table below also offers each team opportunities to share ideas for improvement in distinct categories for leadership development, tactical change, and additional resources. Eventually this will help leaders set priorities for the future.

Ministry Area						
Measureable Outcomes	1. 2. 3. 4.					
Program or Activity	Acceleration (1–10)	Impact (1–10)	Total Score (2–20)	Ideas for Improvement		
				Leadership	Tactics	Resources
1.						
2.						
3.						

Once the ministry team has listed and evaluated their programs and activities using the two principles for a combined score, they can pare the list down for the purpose of overall strategic thinking. All programs or activities that are doing well (i.e., with a combined score of 15–20) are removed from the list. A leadership summit doesn't need to spend time reviewing programs that are doing well, or at least well enough. As long as the vision is clear and the boundaries of trust are honored, a ministry team can reliably manage these programs on its own. The focus of energy in a leadership summit will be on programs and activities that are either struggling or not achieving their full potential.

In a sense, this might be called a "reverse triage." Triage normally describes how an organization segregates extremely weak programs or insoluble problems and concentrates only on the programs that are working well or very well. Here it appears that the most effective programs are being segregated so that a leadership summit can focus on the weaker or less effective programs. Is this a waste of energy?

The answer is no, it is not a waste of energy. The process gives the ministry team authority and responsibility to continue shaping and tweaking very effective programs without interference. In strategic thinking, time is in fact wasted when staff and board leaders meddle in what is already going well. Instead, their valuable time is invested in solving problems that ministry teams can't seem to resolve. More importantly, the staff and board leaders in a retreat can make the difficult decision (often resisted by a ministry team) to simply *terminate* a program.

Let's continue looking at the strategic thinking of St. Anonymous Church leaders and use the worship team as an example. The cluster of teams rating systemic effectiveness for *traction* has done its work, and now each team in the cluster will refine the assessment further. Here I only focus on the work of the worship team. You will recall that four insights from the cluster conversation about systemic effectiveness directly relate to the worship team:

- Some choir and band members seemed more passionate about *performance* than pursuing the overall *vision* of the church to multiply disciples and bless the world in the name of Christ.

- Some lay leaders involved in worship (musicians, liturgists, technicians, etc.) did not feel sufficiently competent to do high-quality ministry or confident to easily share faith.

- There was a clear contrast in worship expectations between lifestyle segments overrepresented in the church but well represented in the community.

- Too many first- and second-time visitors were failing to become involved in church life and mission.

These insights informed the team as they evaluated the various programs associated with worship. Eventually their list of programs and evaluations for *acceleration* and *impact* looked like this.

Ministry Area	Worship (including Sunday worship services and special worship services)					
Measureable Outcomes	1. Sunday worship is a perfect blend of inspiration giving hope for the future, and education giving insight into faith and morality. 2. Occasional worship that celebrates important religious and cultural festivals, and gathers large crowds within which mature Christians can network informally with spiritual seekers.					
Program or Activity	Acceleration (1–10)	Impact (1–10)	Total Score (2–20)	Ideas for Improvement		
				Leadership	Tactics	Resources

9:30 Worship Service	9	8	*17*		
11:00 Worship Service	5	7	12		Life-style Sensi-tivity?	
Choirs	*10*	*5*	*15*			
Bands	4	6	10	Training?		
Preachers & Liturgists	8	5	13		Life-style Sensi-tivity?	
Christmas Eve	9	9	*18*			
Easter Sunrise	4	5	9	Younger Leader-ship?		
Annual Youth Service	7	5	12			More Funding?
Family Sunday	9	9	*18*			
24/7 Open Door Chapel	1	2	3		Termi-nate?	

The leaders of St. Anonymous understood that the programs identified in *italics* above scored 15+ and did not need to be revisited by the staff and board. These were doing very well, and the ministry team could make any improvements. (Note, however, that the choirs were borderline at 15 and next year might need closer evaluation).

The leaders of St. Anonymous saw that a number of programs had total scores between 7 and 15. The relative scores for *acceleration* and *impact* would give clues to further evaluation in the leadership summit, and the team offered some suggested lines of reflection. For example, the programs related to Preachers and Liturgists and 11:00 Worship Service needed to be reviewed in light of different ministry expectations among lifestyle segments. Other programs might be helped by further training, younger leadership, or more funding.

Finally, the leaders of St. Anonymous saw that the program that kept the outside doors to the chapel open seven days a week was not living up to expectations at all. The chapel was little used by church or community members. However, the chapel had long been a sacred cow of the church, and the ministry team felt their hands were tied to do anything about it.

Creative New Ideas

The last step in the assessment is the exploration of creative ideas and new initiatives. Creativity is usually the result of some interaction between activity and reflection. This is why most creative ideas come from the ministry teams rather than from the board.

The ministry teams are active on the ground, in the community, face to face with the real circumstances, interacting with different publics, and empathic with distinct lifestyle segments. At the same time, they monitor demographic trends, understand worldviews, interpret life concerns, and are constantly researching nuances for lifestyle expectations of ministry as they quest for God.

Demographic and lifestyle research can either provide the spark of an idea or the inspiration for innovative design—or both together. Sometimes the research itself suggests a new way to bless the community, and it is reality-tested through focus groups and interview times. Sometimes the research shapes the implementation of a creative idea, and it is reality-tested though prayer walking and listening strategies.

Often it is a demographic trend or psychographic insight that provides the spark for a new idea. For example, ministry teams may discern a trend in the community that opens up new opportunities to bless people in the name of Christ. For example:

- Phase of Life research may uncover increases or decreases in households with preschool children or elementary or high school children; among singles and young adults; among young families or empty-nesters; or among seniors.

- Economic research may reveal upward or downward trends of wealth or poverty, which may parallel housing trends for larger single-family dwellings or apartment complexes, which in turn may parallel educational and occupational trends for advanced education or professional training in white-collar and blue-collar jobs.

- Ethnic, racial, country-of-origin, and primary language trends might suggest long term migrations of populations, and presage the transformation of entire neighborhoods. This can impact retail businesses, grocery store food choices and restaurant menus, public education curricula and extracurricular activities, emergency services, and so on.

When ministry teams see these trends, they can share their suspicions and predictions with other social service, education, or health partners to verify the significance of the research. Then they can start to adapt programs or innovate ideas to respond to changing circumstances.

Often it is lifestyle segment research that provides the inspiration to design new programs. The hiring or redeployment of leadership; new program content, communication methods, facilities, and technologies; and new funding- and financial-management strategies are all shaped in response to changing day-to-day realities in neighborhoods, workplaces, schools, and playgrounds. For example:

- The leadership expectations of growing lifestyle segments will demand the addition of new paid or unpaid staff or additional training and redeployment of existing volunteers and staff.

- Understanding lifestyle will shape the design of new worship alternatives and preaching themes, small group methods and topics, Christian education methods and resources, symbol systems and appropriate technologies, and communication and advertising techniques.

When ministry teams experience changes in the mission field first-hand, they can research lifestyle segment expectations to design relevant tactics. Creativity can be based on more objective observation and research, and free itself from the whims and fancies of individual imaginations.

Let's look again at St. Anonymous Church, following the assessment process of the Worship Team.

In their previous assessment of ongoing programs, the ministry team discerned three programs that scored low for *acceleration* and *impact*: the 11:00 service, the annual youth service, and the annual Easter sunrise service. None of these programs were coming close to realizing the measureable outcomes for worship design in the church.

They realized that the weaknesses in these programs were not new but part of an ongoing decline of effectiveness over several years. The reason must be due to demographic and lifestyle trends in the mission field rather than unexpected glitches in tactic. They probed more deeply in research and expanded their listening strategies in the community. And they focused on several creative ideas.

1. The 11:00 worship service was too similar to the 9:30 worship service, but the lifestyle segments that appreciated a blend of educational-caregiving worship were declining in the mission field. There was no longer a critical mass of population to require two of the same kind of worship service. The ministry team proposed a radical reinvention of the second service to be much more inspirational.

2. Lifestyle segment research and interviews with public education and social service workers revealed that the "youthful population" had changed. Now there were several lifestyle segments that included children and young adults, but they were so different from one another that the expectations of youth could no longer be addressed in a single, annual worship service. The ministry team decided to eliminate the youth service altogether and transform the existing Sunday worship options to be more consistently "youthful" through adjustments to the liturgy and deployment of youth in routine worship leadership.

3. The Easter sunrise service was a theological priority but a practical failure. It was hard to make it truly inspiring and joyous when so few people attended. The worship team considered entering a partnership with a neighboring church in order to combine attendance and improve leadership. Together they could provide funding for high-quality music and make the service more powerful and inspiring.

Of course, ideas are not enough. The worship team understood that they needed to align these changes with the vision and mission of the church, and explain how these initiatives might better achieve measureable outcomes. And they needed to define how these initiatives would improve *acceleration* and *impact*.

The team created a chart similar to the one evaluating ongoing programs, the difference being that this chart focused on anticipating mission results. Note that the team did not have to explain every detail. They provided only what the board needed most to set priorities for the future.

Ministry Area:	Worship (including Sunday worship services and special worship services)						
Measure-able Out-comes:	1. Sunday worship is a perfect blend of inspiration giving hope for the future, and education giving insight into faith and morality. 2. Occasional worship that celebrates important religious and cultural festivals, and gathers large crowds within which mature Christians can network informally with spiritual seekers.						
New Initiative	Antici-pated Accel-eration (1–10)	Antici-pated Impact (1–10)	Total Score (2–20)	Key Prioritization Factors			
				Why	Who	Results	Costs
11:00 In-spirational Worship	9	9	18	More Inspira-tion	Rede-ployed Band Motiva-tional Speakers	Higher atten-dance of lifestyles now under-repre-sented	$5,000 Retrain-ing Preacher
Youth Leaders in All Worship	6	9	15	Include more youth	Current Leaders + Youth	Lower median age of worship	$2,000 for training
Easter Sunrise Merged Worship	10	5	15	Raise profile of major religious event	Two church partners	Higher at-tendance & quality	$3,000 for paid musicians

The chart provided the essential information needed to make the new idea a priority among other programs. While the worship team believed the change of focus for the 11:00 service would improve both *acceleration* and *impact*, they recognized that the other initiatives might be more lop-sided (even though the cumulative score would be high). Youth leaders in every worship service would probably not foment church growth, but it would increase the reach of the church among the more diverse young adult population. A merged Easter sunrise service might not change the world, but it certainly would increase attendance and enthusiasm.

Churches with high trust, clear congregational purpose, and defined measureable outcomes find it much easier to deal with creative ideas, no matter how far out of the box they might be. These churches often pro-vide proscriptive boundaries for action that allow enormous freedom to ministry teams with specific policy limitations, and they often provide ministry areas with large capital pools that leaders can use for innovation without constantly asking permission. Boards are able to focus on vision-ing, long-range planning, community networking, and mentoring emerg-ing leaders. These churches tend to have higher *acceleration* and *impact* in all their programs.

Churches with low trust, foggy congregational purpose or merely ge-neric denominational identity, and no measureable outcomes find it very difficult to deal with creative ideas. Even the smallest innovation requires bureaucratic procedures and approvals. These churches only provide pre-scriptive task lists for implementation and limited funds to do them, re-quiring ministry teams to constantly ask permission and boards to con-stantly micromanage. As boards are drawn into management roles, there is little time for visioning, networking, or mentoring. These churches tend to have lower *acceleration* and *impact* in all their programs.

Regardless of the organizational model of the church, however, cre-ative ideas are still evaluated using the principles of *acceleration* and *impact*. Ministry teams for some churches may be empowered to discern, design, implement, and evaluate by themselves. But they still need to provide a rationale and working strategy for the board to respond to the inevitable questions: *Why are we doing this? Who will lead this? What will result? What will it cost?* The answers must be grounded in demographic research and lifestyle sensitivity. It must be clear that new initiatives are not pet projects or personal passions, but aligned to the vision of the church and relevant to the ever-evolving mission field.

In our example, St. Anonymous Church is a high-trust church that is clear about its purpose and measureable outcomes. Therefore, the worship team simply went ahead with the cancellation of the annual youth service and immediately began training youth to help lead regular worship and reconfigure the leadership teams for all services. It did not require the permission of the board or pastor.

The other two initiatives, however, were more challenging because the *real* cost of discipleship is more than money. The financial cost was not an issue, because expenses for training or part-time contracts were well within the limits of the capital pool available to the worship team. However, these initiatives involved changing attitudes and traditions, along with forming new partnerships and increasing paid staff.

- Any change to Sunday morning worship would likely be stressful for both participants and leaders. Participants who preferred an educational-caregiving service later in the morning would be disappointed and would probably have to come to worship at a different time. The pastor was an expository, but not a motivational, preacher and would have to learn new skills. The band would have to step up to a new standard of quality.

- Merging the sunrise Easter services of two churches was also risky. The vision and mission, core values and bedrock beliefs of the two churches must be compatible. The staff and leadership team must fully respect and cooperate with each other. And paid guest musicians might offend the less capable but longtime volunteers who provided music in the former Easter worship strategy.

The chart above would be forwarded to the planning summit for staff and board to consider among the priorities for the church in the next year.

Once the ministry teams have completed their assessments of ongoing programs and new opportunities, the charts can be used by the board and senior staff to set priorities and define outcomes for the future.

Chapter 5
The Summit of Strategic Thinking

I t should be obvious by now that strategic thinking is a team effort. It is not enough for the pastor to think strategically or for a few board members to think strategically. *All leaders need to think strategically.* In fact, this is a condition of leadership.

Churches often make excuses for their staff and board leaders, or allow staff and board leaders to avoid responsibility for strategic thinking. Staff members may claim to be too "intuitive" for strategic thinking. They convince themselves that it is acceptable to lead solely by charisma or expertise, and expect the church to simply trust their guesswork or blindly obey their instructions. Board members may claim that their role is limited to some specialized knowledge about finance, technology, music, or other expertise, and expect the church to allow them an automatic veto if any plan or idea upsets their assumptions.

It only takes one staff or board leader to undermine the strategic thinking of an entire church. Imagine a formation of geese flying in a straight line from their winter habitat to their summer habitat. All the geese collaborate, taking turns to fly at the point of the V formation. When the leader turns, all turn together. When the leader lands or takes off, all do it together. But imagine what would happen if just one goose decided they did not have to travel as a team and veered one way or another, landing or taking off at different times. Chaos ensues.

When strategic thinking breaks down in a church, the reason is that arrogance has combined with complacency. The pride of one leader is matched by the complacency of the other leaders. And indeed, this is precisely what has happened in so many churches in every tradition over the past decades. Staff and volunteer leaders compete for control of the budget, develop their personal core of volunteers, and manage programs independently of one another. The annual gathering of leaders is usually called a "retreat." As the name implies, the leadership retreat is a time to relax, maintain the appearance of harmony, and reflect on abstract ideas or discuss theological or ideological issues. The retreat doesn't focus on the changing needs of the community or assess the effectiveness of the church. Participants don't leave with clear priorities to improve programs, initiate creative ideas, terminate ineffective tactics, or anticipate the stress of change. They may love each other, appreciate their church tradition, and have more theological insight. But they come unprepared, and they leave unprepared, to lead the church to make a difference in the world.

The annual gathering of leaders is not a "retreat." It is a "summit." It is much the same as the highest level of diplomacy among governments. Clearly, a summit is *not* about micromanagement. It doesn't tinker with programs that are generally doing well. It concentrates on solving unsolvable problems, terminating ineffective tactics, and forwarding creative ideas. The outcome of many retreats was to entrench caution and preserve the status quo. The leadership summit is not about preserving status quo but about aligning ministries to vision and measuring success.

Once again, we see the distinction between strategic *planning* and strategic *thinking*. Strategic planning is a mechanical activity that merely organizes and resources programs led by relatively autonomous leaders. It encourages turf protection and preserves the status quo. Strategic thinking is a diplomatic activity that sets top priorities but also counts the cost of discipleship and anticipates the stress of change. It breaks up fiefdoms, eliminates competition, and celebrates relevance.

The summit is a combination of prioritization and perspiration. Staff, board, and ministry team leaders come together once they have done their homework and summarized their insights. Staff and board members come

prepared with an honest appreciation of the gifts and anxieties of the congregation and are able to interpret the evolving physical, relational, and
spiritual changes of the community. Ministry team leaders come prepared
to brief the gathering on underperforming programs, new ideas, and ineffective tactics; and they can recommend actions and explain the rationale
for them.

The leadership summit answers two questions and concentrates on
two activities. The two questions are, *Were we successful last year? What will
it take to be more successful next year?* The two activities are

- Prioritization: Leaders focus on important programs that are not
  functioning effectively; new ideas; and old and ineffective tactics. First
  they explore *why* they do any program or why they should implement any creative idea; clarify *who* is ready to take responsibility and
  authority to do it; and define the *measureable outcomes* that should
  determine success. Second they explore key issues about *when, how,*
  and *where* programs and ideas will be implemented.

- Perspiration: Leaders discern the true *cost* of the program or idea. The
  true cost of any program involves more than money. It can also involve change to tradition, attitude, organization, leadership, technology, and property. Once leaders understand the real cost of discipleship, they can anticipate the stress that any change might bring.

The timing of the process varies from church to church. Many
churches appoint their leaders and set their budgets at the beginning of
the year, so the leadership summit is usually scheduled in the fall. Other
churches appoint leaders and set budgets in mid-year (June). The summit
is usually scheduled for late winter or spring. Whenever it is scheduled, it
should become an annual routine for the church. Leaders will be *expected
to participate in the* summit as a condition of their office with no exceptions (except for health). This is a crucial moment in the life and work of
a vital church.

The effectiveness of a leadership summit, whether for government
leaders or church leaders, is not only determined by its priorities and di-
plomacies. It is determined by the credibility of the leaders who participate. Credibility is a combination of integrity and alignment. Leaders are

credible if they really do model and articulate the core values and bedrock beliefs of the church, and if their lifestyle and work are clearly aligned to the overarching motivational vision of the church. In other words, the truly represent the Heart Beat and celebrate the Heart Song of the church. They are prepared and eager to discern the *heartburst* for ministry.

It is this credibility that carries strategic thinking to the final stage of delegation. This is often done by staff in collaboration with ministry team leaders. Responsibility and authority is delegated to ongoing or emerging ministry teams to implement what the summit has prioritized. This is often the moment when resources are allocated, budgets are set, and volunteer energy is redistributed. Most importantly, this is the time when measureable outcomes are more clearly defined so that *next year* the leaders can ask and answer these questions: *Were we successful last year? What will it take to be more successful next year?* The questions will have a clear reference point, and the answers will not be a matter of opinion but of objective evaluation.

Leaders who are strategic thinkers must *prepare* for the retreat. They don't just arrive to worry, lament, brainstorm, complain, blame, or micromanage. Strategic thinking begins with "homework." The information they gather will be distributed in advance so the retreat participants can pray and ponder, prioritize, calculate risk, anticipate stress, and delegate authority and responsibility.

- Staff and board do research to understand their evolving membership and their changing community context. As we shall see, research about church and community complement one another. The goal of the church is to mirror in the membership the lifestyle diversity of the community.

- Ministry team leaders review all of the programs and activities within their sphere of influence. As we shall see, they evaluate each program and activity using the twin criteria of *acceleration* and *impact*. They celebrate—but set aside—programs and or activities that are already very effective in growing or strengthening the church, or bringing significant positive change to the community. What they bring to the leadership retreat will be programs and activities that are important but not functioning well; new creative ideas; and programs and activities that have outgrown their usefulness and might be closed.

Such preparation is crucial to successful strategic thinking. If leaders don't do their homework, the leadership retreat will be forced to do "group think." All the research and program assessment will have to be done collectively. This will be exhausting. Some leaders will become bored because they are discussing programs about which they know little and care less. Other leaders will become defensive because people who don't know anything about their sphere of ministry will be meddling and micromanaging. Ultimately, the retreat will never actually do what it is supposed to do, namely, set priorities and make hard decisions.

Many churches require a congregational decision to set an annual budget; employ, redeploy, or dismiss paid staff; or make major changes to facilities. They don't have to know all the details of a plan (unless they don't trust the leaders). If a church member wishes to know more about the plan, the board can readily explain *why* something is being done, *who* will do it, and what *positive outcomes* should result. Ministry team leaders can provide them with specific information about *when, how,* and *where* ministries will occur. They can all explain *how much it will cost* more comprehensively than ever before. Financial planners can build their budgets and fund-raising strategies, but everyone will know the bigger, broader cost of discipleship.

The leadership summit is about teamwork. Therefore, it begins with the celebration of the foundation of trust (the core values and bedrock beliefs that define integrity within and credibility beyond the church that is the "heartbeat" of congregational life and work). It focuses the heartburst for the publics you yearn to bless in the name of Christ. And it ends with the Heart Song that motivates, energizes, and guides all ministries. Everything that happens in a leadership summit is intended to draw a straight line between who we are and who God wants us to become.

The combination of board research and ministry team assessments helps the church set priorities, anticipate costs, and manage the stress of change. Traditionally this happens in a weekend leadership summit. Today the pressures of time and diversity of contexts have caused many variations. Some churches do a leadership summit every year, and others might do it every other year. Some churches do their planning at different times during the year, involving different teams. Whatever the timing might be, however, thriving churches understand that intentional strategic planning is the only way to stay faithful, adaptable, and effective.

You can actually use MissionInsite to decide the right timing for strategic planning for your church and context. The key is to understand the average time of residency in your primary mission field. Some contexts are very stable. Average residency may be as much as five years—which suggests that a church only needs to do a major leadership summit every five years. However, in our increasingly mobile society, the average time of residency is much shorter (as little as a few months). That suggests churches should do strategic thinking annually. I find it increasingly common for churches to alternate minor and major initiatives for strategic planning every other year.

Note especially that the timing for leadership summits is based on the average time of residency *for the primary mission field—not the church membership.* The experience of member households doesn't reflect the realities of the mission field. The average length of residency *for member households* is often much longer than *mission field households.* Indeed, members have often lived in a context and associated with the same circle of friends for so long that they actually don't see the change that is happening around them. Planning is based on the experience of the mission field, not the church.

The summit should always be held *outside* of the church building but *inside* the mission field. Hold it outside the church building because this literally takes leaders "out of the box." Their minds and imaginations automatically break free from compulsions to maintain property at all costs or simply protect heritage without vision. On the other hand, always hold the meeting *inside* the primary mission field. Don't go to the denominational camp. Don't travel from the city to seclude yourselves in the woods, and don't travel from the country to seclude yourselves in the city. Surround yourselves with the lifestyle segments in the primary mission field that God has commanded you to bless in the name of Christ. When you gaze out the window, take a coffee break, go for a walk to clear your minds, or overhear noises from outside the room, you want to experience the subtle pressure of the mission.

Whenever you do it, make it required. Leadership summits are not optional. Participation is a condition of leadership. The summit should be placed on the calendar well in advance, and no excuse, except illness, should be acceptable for failure to attend. No holidays or family gatherings (including weddings, births, and deaths) should get in the way.

When a promising disciple excused himself from service, saying, "Lord, first let me go and bury my father," Jesus replied sternly, "Follow me and let the dead bury their own dead" (Matt 8:21-22 CEB). This sounded hard then, and it sounds hard today, but it points to the power of the vision and what is ultimately important. It is extremely rare that, given sufficient lead time, employees are unable to negotiate with employers for time off. Even business trips can be scheduled earlier or later to make time for the church —if you really, really believe it is important. And it is.

If leaders make excuses or beg off from attending the leadership summit, it is a clear sign that deep in their hearts they don't think the vision is really important. It is only moderately important. And you should never have anyone in leadership in the church who thinks that the vision is only moderately important. You only want leaders who believe the vision is absolutely important. Attending the summit is an expectation and condition of leadership.

There are four questions that always need to be answered about leadership summits.

Who Participates in a Leadership Summit?

The summit is not a large group. Twenty people are more than enough. They are, of course, the most broadly credible and officially sanctioned leaders of the church. These include *senior* staff (i.e., the staff or volunteers who oversee the four or five key disciple-making ministry areas of the church); the board (i.e., the six or seven spiritual leaders who mentor others, model faith, know the mission field, and do long-range planning); and selected operational leaders (who oversee property, funding, and communication). The senior pastor leads the summit, although in large churches it may be co-led by an executive minister.

The best summits are large enough to include key leaders for all the subsystems of congregational life and mission but small enough to make decisions efficiently. Ministry team leaders may come and go if and when they are required to interpret a program change or explain a creative idea. Most members don't attend, regardless of their age or seniority. Never include participants who are merely representatives of a particular group based on age, gender, or faction. Lobbyists are not helpful.

What Resources Are Essential for Participants to Have?

Successful ceramic tiling requires that the first tile be set exactly right. If the first tile is set perfectly, every other tile will follow the pattern. In order to set that first tile well, the worker must ensure that the first tile is flawless and square; understand the contours of the surface to anticipate cracks, corners, and special cuts; and draw grid lines to cover the entire floor.

The participants in a summit embody the very identity and purpose of the congregation. Collectively they are the first "tile" in the planning process, and they need to be properly prepared for all subsequent work to be effective.

- Equip participants with a clear summary of vision and mission, core values and bedrock beliefs, and overall measureable outcomes for each ministry area of the church.

- Leaders must be empathic to *their changing mission field*. They need to have a comprehensive sensitivity to all of the major lifestyle segments, and the diversity of micro cultures, that exist within the primary mission field of the church. That mission field is always defined by the average commute people in the zip code are willing to make to work and shop. Leaders need to know the key demographic trends that are under way now, and will continue to unfold, in the next five to ten years. If MissionInsite tools are not available, other forms of board research should be provided, such as social surveys or books and articles about contemporary culture or social disruptions.

- The most essential resources from MissionInsite research include the ComparativeInsite Report and a summary spreadsheet that provides phase-of-life trends and comparative ministry expectations of the major lifestyle segments represented in both primary mission field and church membership. There may be specific demographic and psychographic data that the board considers especially significant at this time.

- Leaders must understand *program options and opportunities*. They need to have a complete list of emerging ideas and ongoing programs that will be reviewed during the summit so that they can begin to pray and ponder mission alignment and effectiveness in advance of the meeting. They rarely examine relatively effective programs and focus on struggling programs and new ideas, but they still need the big picture. All that matters is the gospel; everything else is tactics.

- The most essential resources from ministry team assessments include the evaluation charts for each subsystem (*traction* and *steering*) and the evaluation charts from each team regarding ongoing programs and creative ideas relevant to their sphere of influence. There may be specific information regarding stories or perspectives that emerge from mission team listening strategies and contextual experiences.

All this should be summarized in a brief that is in the hands of the summit participants at least two weeks prior to the event. They should then incorporate this information into daily prayer and reflection. Metaphorically speaking, this spiritual amalgam of perception and prayer is the "glue" that will make the first tile (and all subsequent tiles) "adhere" to the mission field and transform the culture of the zip code.

What Exactly Does the Summit Accomplish?

Ministry teams forward their evaluation charts for subsystems of *traction* and *steering*, and evaluation charts of ongoing programs and creative ideas. However, they clearly indicate which programs are doing well and *don't* need to be included in the conversations of the leadership summit. Ministry teams also clearly indicate those creative new ideas that are well within their responsibility and authority to implement without further permission.

Low-trust churches that are foggy about vision and measureable outcomes usually handle these "exclusions" of programs and creative ideas from consideration during the summit as a "consent docket." This means that approval for a cluster of programs and ideas is automatically assumed and confirmed in a single decision. The summit participants then spend time on other programs and new ideas.

High-trust churches that are clear about vision and measureable outcomes don't even bother with the formalities of a consent docket. They are confident that the goals and boundaries that define ministry team mandates are clear, that a ministry team leader can be trusted, and that ongoing systems of evaluation and accountability can be managed by the senior pastor or senior staff. Nevertheless, summit participants can make exceptions. There may be a program or idea that they think needs more thought or discussion, and it is often at that point that ministry team leaders are asked to temporarily join the discussion.

What, then, does the summit accomplish if it is not bogged down in second-guessing ministry teams or revisiting old debates? There are six major concerns, and six basic results that emerge from a leadership summit.

Measurable Outcomes

Summit participants must evaluate success. It is their responsibility to determine if the ministry teams have succeeded, approximated, or failed to achieve the outcomes set before them. This is not about praise or blame. It is about effectiveness. If an outcome is only partially achieved, the senior staff and board need to understand if the goal was unrealistic, the leaders insufficiently trained, or the tactics imperfectly conceived and implemented.

One result of the leadership summit is that ministry teams have new or revised measureable outcomes that they will use to improve programs, initiate new ideas, or terminate ineffective tactics.

Systemic Changes

Leadership summit participants are particularly concerned about the dynamics of *traction* and *steering*. This is really about sustaining and encouraging teamwork. The programs of hospitality, worship, small groups, and caregiving and the programs of Christian education, outreach, evangelism, and property and finance are not developed in isolation of each other. This is a common problem in institutions known as "program silos." Changes in one ministry area often impact changes in other ministry areas in unforeseen ways.

A second result of the summit is that ministry teams will work together for a common goal and not block or compete with one another.

Insoluble Problems

The programs that *are* discussed by the summit participants are usually programs that are not fully effective. Either they aren't delivering *acceleration* or they aren't delivering *impact*—or both. These are also problem programs that the relevant ministry team can't seem to solve. This means that these problems tend to be *chronic* rather than *acute*. Problem programs don't tend to come to a leadership summit when they don't perform for the first time but rather because they seem to need help all the time.

A third result of the summit is that specific programs are improved, revised, or occasionally terminated.

Ministry Priorities

Every church has limited resources, and every mission field has changing circumstances. The priorities of a church two years ago may not and perhaps should not be the priorities of a church in the future. Internally, this often involves slaying sacred cows that undermine the effectiveness of a church. Externally, this often involves new or different heartbursts to address emerging (or even unpopular) issues or particular lifestyle segments (large or small, growing or diminishing).

A fourth result of the summit is that the framework of ministry is reshaped or the focus of ministry is revised. Sometimes this implies significant changes in staff configurations, property acquisition or development, and capital campaigns.

Cost of Discipleship

Participants in a leadership summit tend to become involved in creative new ideas only in specific ways. They *don't* spend time discussing the details of when, how, or where a creative new idea might be initiated. That is left to the ministry team. They *do* spend time discussing the true cost of discipleship. The cost of change involves much more than money. It involves changes to attitude, tradition, leadership, organization, property, and technology—in addition to money. This is the first part of "risk management."

A fifth result of the summit is that the church manages risk and cost. Leaders understand how far they can go and how radical they can be.

Anticipated Stress

Another way participants in a summit become involved in creative new ideas is by anticipating stres and preparing to address stress in healthy and faithful ways. Once they know the true cost of discipleship (the seven cost centers that are involved in any change), they can predict where, when, and with whom stress will occur.

A sixth result of the summit is that stress can be resolved in appropriate ways. A healthy balance of harmony and risk can be sustained.

You can see that the result of a leadership summit is a plan—but not the kind of plan many traditional church members assume. This is not a plan that confirms every program and manages how it will be done. This is a plan for aligning ministries to vision, evaluating success, encouraging teamwork, solving problems, setting priorities, counting costs, and anticipating stress. The management details can be trusted to the teams.

What Does the Agenda Look Like?

Once you understand the expected results of a leadership summit, you get a pretty good idea of what the agenda looks like. Of course, how the time is apportioned in the agenda may vary from year to year (responding to emerging issues and changing circumstances). The basic pattern, however, looks like this:

- *Pray:* Pray specifically for courage within the congregation, and sensitivity to the mission field beyond the congregation. Prayer is a combination of thanksgiving and intercession.

- *Celebrate Vision:* Celebrate the Heart Song. Sing the theme song and meditate on the inspiring image. Motivate leaders toward selflessness and sacrifice. Inspire them to stretch their imaginations.

- *Celebrate Trust:* Feel the Heart Beat. Review the congregational consensus and Christian accountability of shared positive behavioral expectations (core values) and shared convictions (bedrock beliefs) that unite and strengthen the church.

- *Focus Mission:* Review the significance of demographic trends, lifestyle expectations, and psychographic benchmarks.

- *Monitor Systems:* Ensure that the church is getting efficient traction and traveling in the right direction.

- *Evaluate Programs:* Improve ongoing programs, initiate new ideas, or terminate ineffective tactics.

- *Set Priorities and Define Outcomes:* Set the goals for the next period of one to five years of ministry.

- *Delegate Authority and Responsibility:* Empower ministry teams to achieve results in any way they can within the boundaries of the policies of the board.

The flow of the summit varies according to contextual changes, spiritual discernment, and changing resources. Occasionally, the emphasis might be on revising the values and beliefs, vision and mission of the church. Depending on the speed of cultural change, the emphasis might be on analyzing the mission field and adapting programs. Routinely the emphasis may be on solving problems and redefining outcomes.

Once a church becomes familiar with research and listening tools, and the principles of program assessment, preparation for the summit takes about six months.

- The board uses MissionInsite to update People Plot, monitor key demographic trends, and compare proportionate lifestyle segment representation between mission field and membership.

- The ministry teams use MissionInsite to target listening strategies, compare ministry expectations among lifestyle segments, and evaluate *acceleration* and *impact*.

The summit brings research and assessment together. Vision is clear and trust is high. Ministry teams have provid careful assessments for *acceleration* and *impact* for ongoing programs, recommend changes, and present creative new ideas. As the church looks to the future, the summit focus is primarily on improving several chronic problems in traction and steering, improving specific programs related to worship, and setting new outreach priorities.

Chapter 6

The Outcomes of
Strategic Thinking

S trategic thinking is all about drawing a straight line from identity to outcome. Organizational identity is defined by trust and vision. Organizational success is defined by measureable outcomes. Everything that happens in between—community research, spiritual discernment, and church assessment —are crucial steps along the way.

Strategic *thinking* is different from strategic *planning* because it focuses on outcomes, not processes; and success, not tactics. The temptation for many churches today, however, is to become obsessed with tactics. This is because from the very beginning they are unclear about their identity. Lack of trust means that all forward thinking becomes a negotiation or competition. Every tactic needs to be micromanaged to satisfy all of the factions or personalities of the church. Lack of vision leads to program silos and turf protection, and creative thinking never goes beyond the boundaries of traditional "sacred" programming. Churches become so absorbed in strategic *planning* that they never question their lack of success. Or to put it another way, success is only measured by sustained harmony rather than effective ministry.

Strategic thinkers can't allow themselves to get stuck on tactics. They aren't concerned about *how* things get done, nor even about *what* things get done. They are concerned about why things get done and about *what outcomes* should result no matter what is done. It's not that

115

tactics are unimportant. These can be delegated to trusted teams who are able to innovate ideas and use resources in whatever way works. It is more important for them to accelerate church growth and change the world than preserve harmony and protect turf. Indeed, true unity doesn't depend on tactical agreements but on shared identity and the celebration of success.

Strategic *thinkers* understand that no program (especially no program silo) is sacred. For example, if the traditional Sunday school is still useful (as it is in many places in the Midwest), then strategic thinkers will trust the traditional Sunday school superintendent and his or her team to tweak it rather than waste their time micromanaging it. However, if the traditional Sunday school is no longer useful (as it is in many places in the Northeast or Northwest), the strategic thinkers will simply cancel the Sunday school, dismiss or reassign the superintendent, and invest their time thinking of an alternative way to educate Christians. For strategic thinkers, the only thing sacred is the mission. Everything else is mere tactics.

Strategic *thinking* is essential. Strategic *planning* is optional. Planning can be delegated to trusted teams. And indeed, even they may not do strategic planning. Many authors, consultants, and leaders have pointed out that fixed programs, rigid timelines, itemized budgets, and work routines are often unhelpful in a time of fast change and unpredictable events. Better to trust tactics to a team capable of quick thinking and timely creativity than a committee with slow deliberations and engrained habits.

Ironically, the success of an organization today actually depends on the failures of its teams. It is only when teams experiment with tactics, fail, learn, and innovate until they get results that the organization itself becomes relevant and effective. For the success of a church, tactical failures are not only an option but a necessity. Strategic *thinking*, not strategic *planning*, is crucial. Organizational growth and mission impact are only possible if leaders follow a straight line from identity to outcome. If that fails, the church fails, no matter how perfect their tactics might be.

If that succeeds, the church succeeds, no matter what failure might occur along the way.

Remember that there are two major goals for every leadership summit. The first goal is to set priorities. The second is to measure risk and anticipate stress. The leadership summit is about *prioritization* and *perspiration*.

Remember that the ministry teams have already completed their own evaluations for programs within their sphere of influence—and may have investigated creative new ideas. All this is forwarded to the summit participants, but the focus of the summit is clearly on *underperforming ongoing programs* or *creative ideas*. Programs and creative ideas that are already effective or successful are left with the teams. Why waste time with micromanagement?

And remember that there may be exceptions. The summit participants may want to take a closer look at borderline programs. They may also want to re-evaluate creative ideas in light of changing organizational priorities or because the cost of discipleship and potential stress call for closer scrutiny.

Prioritization

Whether the summit agenda evaluates a whole list of programs at one time or concentrates on specific programs and new ideas, the template for evaluation is basically the same. The chart below provides the key steps and the order in which they are taken. Of course, leaders can use this template at any time, in any ministry area, for any program or idea in order to plan effectively, define costs, and anticipate stress.

Ministry teams often use this template to provide a total score for *acceleration* and *impact* that will help them balance ministries that combine to grow the church *and* change the world. Summit participants can go further. They can use the template over and over again for each program in a ministry area and use it to set priorities. Generally speaking, only programs that score high for *acceleration* and/or *impact* should be given resources for implementation.

Program or Creative Idea			
The Point	**The Boundaries**	**Major Cost Centers** (High, Medium, Low)	**Stress Management**
Why:	**When?** Begin? Schedule? Evaluation? Closure?	Tradition: Attitude:	Personal Growth:
Who:	**How?** Training? Technology? Expertise?	Leadership: Organization:	Accountability:
		Property:	Mission Sensitivity:
Anticipated Results:	**Where?** Environment? Accessibility? Relationships?	Technology: Finance:	Lifestyle Adjustments:
Step 5	Acceleration:	Impact:	Total Score:
Step 6	**Delegation:** Leader(s) to take authority and responsibility for implementation		
Step 7	**Termination:** Date for evaluation and/or closure		

The Point

Three questions always come first. If any program or new idea fails to answer any one of these three questions, it should be removed from the table and not even be considered in the summit conversations. You might say that this is the "first cut" that determines what programs or ideas actually come to the attention of strategic thinkers in the leadership summit. This rule should be applied *without exception*.

No ongoing program should be considered further, even if it has a long history or enjoys wide popularity in the church, if these three questions can't be answered satisfactorily.

No new idea should be considered further, even if it is encouraged by the denomination or is favored by particularly influential people, if these three questions cannot be answered satisfactorily.

This radical action doesn't necessarily mean that the program or idea is bad. It may well be an important program or great idea. However, if it fails to answer the first three questions, it simply can't be implemented. It will *necessarily* fail. The program or creative idea will be set aside by strategic thinkers and referred to ongoing prayer and reflection, and they will not waste time debating it or waste resources implementing it.

Too many church leaders try to "force" the church to implement strategies for which the church is unprepared. This "top-down" approach imposes programs and then scrambles to justify them, recruit leaders to implement them, and invent standards for evaluation down the road. This approach compromises the congregational consensus of values, beliefs, vision, and mission for the congregation. It also encourages intimidating controllers to use power politics to set congregational agendas. And it results in burnout and reduced numbers of volunteers. This top-down approach only worked in the Christendom era when culture valued Christian institutions and offices, and when volunteers were dutiful and plentiful. Today, leaders recognize that ministry and mission strategies must bubble up from the spiritual growth of the people in the context of high trust and clear purpose.

Why?

Previously I described how congregational vision is often expressed as a *theme song* or *inspiring image* (in addition to any propositional *mission statement*). Strategic thinkers use these as reference points to evaluate and prioritize new ideas and ongoing programs. The very first question to be asked of any ongoing program or creative new idea is *why* the congregation should do it. Will it really help the congregation accomplish its mission? Will it encourage the congregation to fulfill the vision God has revealed?

This is why strategic thinkers have spent so much time defining, refining, and celebrating core values, beliefs, vision, and mission; and why they spent even more time studying the facts and trends of the mission field. Their answer isn't merely subjective. It doesn't emerge simply from their personal perspective (preferences, like and dislikes, tastes, and biases). Their answer is really objective. It emerges from their clarity about congregational identity and purpose, and empathy with the lifestyle segments of the mission field, that lies beyond personal idiosyncrasies.

This is why strategic thinkers should be chosen as much for their spiritual maturity, self-discipline, and personal passion for the mission of the church as for any specific skill in organization or resource management. The best way for them to answer this question is through personal meditation prior to the summit and group prayer as they consider each program or idea.

Vision is always connected to *people* rather than *programs*. Precisely who will receive or benefit from the program or creative idea? Paul had a vision of a Macedonian pleading for his team to "come over...and help us" (Acts 16:9). The Macedonian is a definable, describable demographic. The Macedonians live, dress, and eat in a particular way. They speak a specific language and follow specific traditions. They appreciate their own kind of music and express themselves through unique art forms. They have specific physical and spiritual needs, nuanced for their specific environments. So who is *your* "Macedonian"? Who appears in those leaders' dreams, begging them for help? Who do they want to reach?

It is important for strategic thinkers to be as specific as possible. General references to "the public" or "seekers" won't do. There are many publics and many kinds of seekers. It is most helpful if mission teams can specify lifestyle portrait they hope to reach. The "Macedonians" with whom leaders wish to be in dialogue can be vividly pictured. If Saint Paul had a video camera he might have taken their picture in order to describe them to the Jerusalem council. Strategic thinkers literally attach still photos or streaming video to focus the alignment between vision and blessing.

It is astonishing how often churches proceed to implement programs and ideas without really knowing why they should do it. They do it because the denomination or some other outside authority wants them to do it; they do it to make some individual or group happy; they do it because it seems traditional and they always did it in the past; or they do it because church members are aging and lifestyles are changing, and programs match their personal neediness. The church never pauses to ask if program choices deliver God's purpose to redeem the world, multiply disciples, or bless strangers with a peculiar grace.

This single, crucial step in the planning process is what rescues a church from becoming terminally inward in its focus. It requires a prior clarity about what exactly the mission and vision of a particular church is. Church members ages 12 to 99 can now hold church leaders accountable to a standard of success that lies beyond personal neediness or self-centered preference. Perhaps even more importantly, the general public can hold the church accountable for a mission that transcends institutional survival. The credibility of the organization depends on the answer to this question more than anything else. Competency will be secondary. Purposefulness is everything.

Who?

Once strategic thinkers have evaluated mission alignment, the second question involves leadership and recipients. It always takes at least two to make a conversation, and the success of a program or creative idea is more likely if that conversation is expanded to four.

The question of leadership always takes precedence over questions of tactics. A program or creative idea may have excellent or obvious tactics, but without leadership it will never succeed. A program or creative idea may not have clear tactics, but leaders can always innovate the way forward. No program or creative idea should ever be initiated (or even be given the time and energy for consideration) if from the beginning there are no clear leaders.

There should be at least *two* leaders for every ongoing program or creative idea. This is in keeping with the post-Christendom, bottom-up world. One person will likely be overburdened or become a lone ranger and eventually burn out. Two leaders can support each other and create a team.

These leaders are people who are *passionate* and *called* to the ongoing program or new idea. They are passionate in that they find real joy and self-fulfillment in the work. They are called in that they are willing to stake time and energy, embark on a continuous learning process, and make personal sacrifices for the work. These are not just advocates. They are not people who merely encourage or endorse the program or idea but prefer that someone else be hired or appointed to implement it. These leaders will *take the lead.* They are willing to be held accountable for results that confirm the core values and beliefs of the church and align with the mission and vision of the church.

These leaders will find, train, and evaluate others (paid or unpaid) to help fulfill the program or implement the idea. They will probably not do it all by themselves. Yet they will take responsibility and authority to lead a team to define the mission purpose of a program or idea, design appropriate tactics, implement those tactics, and evaluate success. If the pastor or board members have questions about a program or creative idea, they will know who to ask.

What does a leader look like? The planning team needs to have some criteria in mind in order to have confidence in their assessment. I have already said that true leaders will have both passion and calling for the program or new idea. In addition, leaders will have:[8]

- Mission Attitude: True leaders align their lifestyle to God's mission. It is not just that they understand and celebrate congregational vision and purpose. They have experienced the power of God that has changed them, is shaping them, and will lead them to follow Christ to bless the world. A mission attitude is not only an understanding of God's purpose but a sense of urgency to be about God's work.

- Spiritual Habits: True leaders will practice spiritual habits daily, weekly, and through the year. These may include daily prayer and meditation, Bible reading or study, regular worship attendance, and other practices through which their lifestyles are shaped by God. Their spiritual discipline is uniquely customized for their lifestyles. It is not generic, artificial, and burdensome. It is personal, natural, and joyous.

8. I describe these in more detail in my book *Spirited Leadership* (Atlanta: Chalice Press, 2006).

- High Integrity: True leaders will understand and model the core values and beliefs of the church. They won't willingly or unthinkingly contradict them, and if they mistakenly do so, they will know it is wrong and correct their behavior. Furthermore, true leaders will understand and live within basic policies of the church regarding decision-making habits or executive limitations that protect safety and encourage personal growth. They will live up to their accountability in the community of faith.

- Relevant Skills: True leaders will have skills relevant to the ongoing program or creative idea, or be willing to acquire them through strategies for learning or training. They aim toward a standard of excellence and are prepared to coach and equip others to achieve that standard of quality.

- Commitment to Team: True leaders surrender ego to the combined power and mutual support of a team. They work cooperatively, accept accountability, and support one another to become better servants. Essentially, they help one another focus mission attitude, practice spiritual habits, live up to standards of high integrity, and learn new skills.

Of course, no one is perfect. Even the apostles had their failings and struggles. But leaders always focus on the upward call, press on in loyal service, and help each other in personal growth and transformation.

Once again, it is astonishing how often churches perpetuate ongoing programs or initiate new ideas without any clear leadership. They assume a committee can simply be appointed and that out of a sense of institutional duty and pooled ignorance, effective and lasting ministry will result. Pastor, board, and core leaders never quite know who to ask if they have a question. Nobody is sure whether volunteers will show up or suddenly be "too busy" when the time of implementation arrives. Nobody pushes for a standard of quality. Nobody measures success or failure with any confidence.

Churches often hire staff, elect officers, or appoint volunteers as "leaders" without any assurance that they will live within boundaries and align to the vision, practice spiritual habits, or develop relevant skills. In short, they appoint "coordinators" rather than true leaders. Coordinators are generalists who simply assemble resources and move people around. They facilitate, administrate, and enable but are helpless in real problem solving and useless for personal motivation or real self-sacrifice. Every congregation has a limited pool of these generalists who can be moved from committee to committee or from one ministry area to another without having any particular passion or calling to anything. None of them qualify as "leaders" in the context of strategic thinking.

Unless there are leaders, the program or creative idea will not be taken further in the planning process. There must be two leaders, and these must be true leaders and not just coordinators. The program or idea may still be great, but it can't be implemented unless there are true leaders to do it. Pastor, staff, and other spiritual leaders will need to continue casting the vision for this program or new idea like a fly fisherman casting a line into the river. Eventually, prayerfully, someone may rise to the bait. More profoundly, the person who takes the bait will find that they themselves are "hooked" on God's project. They are captured and captivated by a particular ministry or mission that will accomplish the vision of the church.

Anticipated Results

The final question that must be answered in order to survive the first cut in the planning process requires the definition of anticipated, measurable results. It is perhaps the most crucial question of all.

What should happen? Exactly how will success be evaluated? What positive personal or social changes should be visible if true leaders perfectly implement the program or idea?

Of course, this step is often the greatest challenge for many teams. Church people are often unnecessarily upset by it. They think that such quantification diminishes ministry. They think that reducing mission to numbers renders it shallow. Ministry and mission is *qualitative* rather than *quantitative*. In actual practice, though, it isn't possible to deepen the quality of mission without quantifying mission results in some way. The lack of quantifiable measurements of success actually allows churches to plateau at relatively shallow depths of spirituality and relatively minor impact in mission outreach.

The earliest church understood the need to measure results very clearly. The apostles always celebrated the fact that converts were constantly joining their Christian communities; that deacons, elders, and other Christian missionaries were multiplying; that people were actually being healed; that children and adults were actually learning more about scripture; or that pagan institutions and practices were actually changing under the impact of the gospel.

As indicated earlier, there are three basic ways, anticipated mission results can be measured for any ongoing program or creative idea:

- Measure actual numbers of participants, attendance, contributions, and so on (often revealed through statistics managed by the church).

- Measure signs or significations that hidden transformation is happening (often revealed through stories gathered from focus groups and listening strategies).

- Measure perceptions from social service agencies, ecumenical colleagues, para-church nonprofits, or others (often revealed through feedback gathered from interviews).

It should be possible to specify anticipated results for any ongoing program or creative idea, no matter what it might be, in one or more of these categories. In order to make this clearer, some examples can be drawn from worship, spiritual growth, prayer ministry, and outreach.

First, measure success with actual numbers. Count the participants; add up the contributions; identify the network connections. Establish reasonable targets that might be achieved if the program or idea is implemented effectively within a reasonable time frame.

- The success of a monthly healing worship service, for example, can be measured by how many people attend. More accurately, it might measure the growing percentage of the broken public who participate in the healing worship service over one or two years.

  Perhaps the service attracts ten people at the beginning and grows to one hundred at the end of the year. Perhaps the healing worship service is implemented in a neighborhood surrounded by hospitals and medical facilities where it is estimated that ten thousand broken people temporarily reside every month, and the healing worship service draws an increasing percentage of that population. Perhaps success can be measured by how many hospitals, medical centers, or counseling services network with the healing service to refer patients to it. Even more profoundly, success might be measured by the number of people who are, in fact, healed through the experience of the healing worship service.

- The success of a Bible study program, for example, can be measured by how many newcomers join over a period of time, how many students graduate to an advanced level of Bible study, or how many worshipers bring Bibles to worship and read them during the liturgy.

Perhaps the Bible study begins with five people, and grows to twelve within six months. Perhaps the first group births three additional groups over a period of two years or the group leader mentors three more group leaders within eighteen months. Even more profoundly, perhaps the Bible study program eventually prepares several new lay pastors who begin alternative worship services. All these are measurable results that indicate the success of the ministry.

- The success of a prayer ministry, for example, can be measured by how many people join the prayer chain; how long they participate; how many newcomers they invite to join; or the increasing volume of prayer requests coming to the ministry.

Perhaps the prayer chain began with a small group of eight people who covenant together to pray for members in special need over six months. They invite six new participants in the first year and eventually expand the prayer chain into four teams rotating responsibilities each quarter for constant prayer support. Meanwhile, prayer requests that were originally balanced 80/20 between church members and nonmembers have rebalanced to about 50/50. Such measurable results will indicate the success of the prayer chain.

- The success of a food bank, for example, can be measured in how many people use its services; how many donors provide resources; or how many children, seniors, families, or single-parent households are fed each month.

Perhaps the food bank begins with voluntary offerings of canned and dry goods once a month stored in a church closet and distributed Saturday mornings by a small group. Demand rapidly increases because the need is so great. Volunteers increase. Donors from various downtown businesses multiply. Within eighteen months, the food bank is out of the closet and into rented space at the strip mall; a volunteer lawyer is working on nonprofit status; participants are now tracked to various zip codes; and large grocery stores and bakeries are donating unsold and still fresh food. Such measurable results will help food bank leaders plan for future space and apply for future funding.

These are all ways in which churches measure success with actual numbers. Faithful Christians will immediately ask if this is the *only* viable way to measure success, and the answer is certainly not. What if the healing worship service, small group, or prayer chain never grows beyond twenty participants? What if the food bank never expands beyond the closet in the church basement? Does that *necessarily* mean it is a failure? No, but it does beg closer scrutiny by faithful church leaders.

Strategic thinkers can also anticipate results by measuring signs that hidden transformation is happening. What stories should be heard if the ministry is truly successful? What observable, positive social changes might indicate that even a small ministry is having a dramatic impact? Look at the same examples.

- The healing worship service may be small, but success is revealed in the stories of physical, mental, emotional, relational, or spiritual transformation that are told frequently within and beyond the church. There may be a buzz in the community about the power of the experience. Health care professionals are aware of the integrity and therapeutic relevance of the liturgy. Indeed, the incidents of addiction and suicide have been reduced in the zip code over two years; police interventions for domestic violence have gone down; or funeral directors regularly refer grieving individuals to the church.

- The Bible study and the prayer chain may be limited to a small group of people, but success is revealed in the profound spiritual growth of the participants who are now leading mission in other ways. Sermons are more educational and reasonably assume greater biblical literacy among participants. Board and committee meetings run more smoothly and are more intentionally connected to vision. The body of the church seems more serene and focused; worship attendance in general has grown; staff leaders feel more affirmed; or stories about the power of prayer in daily living are repeated during coffee hour. Cooperative community church projects seem more successful and multiply.

- The food bank may be small, but the stories about life-saving help for families in poverty or sudden emergency are powerful. Personal relationships between church members and individuals in desperate situations have increased, and the entire congregation is more aware of economic and demographic trends in the zip code. Other church programs for evangelism or for outreach to children and seniors have become more sensitive to survival issues and practical support for the necessities of life. Other community food banks are less burdened and are appreciative of congregational efforts.

When strategic thinkers anticipate that certain stories will be heard or specific community trends will be altered, they can identify the need to do research. Stories can be listed and catalogued. Trends can be graphed over a period of time and compared to previous years. If there are no stories to be heard, parallel trends to explore, or other significations that a ministry is transforming people in hidden ways, faithful leaders will explore yet another way to measure success.

Finally, measure success by gathering the perceptions, opinions, or perspectives of church members and the general public. These can be general surveys, focus groups, or specific interviews with church and community leaders.

- Leaders for the healing worship service can reasonably be expected to survey church members and selected health networks. Are they even aware of the worship service? If so, what stories have they heard? What is their perception of the mission, integrity, quality, and acceptance of the worship experience? When the healing worship leaders claim certain core values and bedrock faith convictions, do they live up to them? Do specific social service and health care providers recommend the worship experience or not?

- Bible study and prayer-chain leaders can be reasonably expected to gather similar perspectives from denominational and ecumenical sources, and from the spiritually yearning public. Are people aware of the Bible study opportunity? Is the curriculum respected? Are the leaders credible? Is the study aligned well with the vision and mission of the church? Are people hesitant about attending? Do people drop out? Why? Do the regular participants see that the Bible study has changed their own daily lives and service patterns? How?

- Food bank leaders can be expected to network with other social service agencies in the region. They will create focus groups to gather perspective from diverse groups of clients (single parents, unemployed or disabled adults, seniors, etc.). They can do simple surveys in shopping malls and outside grocery stores to identify the changing needs of the public.

In each of these three ways, strategic thinkers expect to measure success. No program or ministry should go forward in the planning process unless there is clarity about what the marks of success would look like or how success will be measured.

If strategic thinkers are not rigorous in this expectation now, then church leaders will find themselves in acrimonious debates and facing unnecessarily stressful decisions in the future. Every program, good or bad, has advocates. There will always be individuals who favor one program over another. If the church has no means to measure success—numerical growth, great stories and signs, or positive perceptions and endorsements—they have no leverage to change program direction or cancel ineffective ministries. They waste money and volunteer energy appeasing the personal opinions of a few. They reduce the credibility of the church in the community by supporting irrelevant or ineffective programs. The pool of money, energy, and community openness is exhausted, and creative new ideas struggle to be born.

Recall the example of St. Anonymous Church. The summit combined the research of the board and the assessment of the ministry teams.

- Board research and examination of the ComparativeInsite Report revealed that specific lifestyle segments in the mission field were over- and underrepresented in church membership. The church was addressing the spiritual yearnings and meeting the ministry expectations of some lifestyle segments but not of others.

- Meanwhile, ministry teams responsible for *traction* evaluated effectiveness and raised concerns about how many first- and second-time

visitors failed to make a permanent connection with the church.
Later, when the worship team evaluated the programs within its
sphere of influence, there were concerns raised about the failure of the
11:00 a.m. worship service to grow in attendance.

Summit participants were able to see a connection. They realized that
the *purposes* of the 9:30 and 11:00 a.m. worship services were redundant,
duplicating efforts to bless the same publics and ignoring the needs of
other lifestyle segments. They recognized that they already had a team
of worship designers and musicians with passion and skills to bless the
underrepresented lifestyle segments in unique ways. They agreed with
the worship team recommendation to radically refocus and redesign the
11:00 a.m. worship service to bless new people. More first- and second-
time visitors would connect permanently with the church, and more stories of personal transformation would be recorded from the mission field.

It should be apparent that the first cut in a leadership summit is often
precisely what strategic *planners* don't do. In fact, they do the opposite.
They completely ignore questions about rationale, leadership, and outcomes and focus entirely on questions about tactics and resources. They
approve pet projects, protect "sacred" traditional programs unquestion-
ingly, delay the smallest innovations, and second-guess the tactical innovations of any given team.

Strategic thinkers have their priorities right. Any program or creative
idea that a team can't justify with a clear explanation of *why* it should be
done, *who* will lead it, and *what results* can be anticipated should be removed from the agenda of the leadership summit. Strategic thinkers don't
waste time on them.

The Boundaries

Strategic thinkers cannot, and should not, micromanage ministry teams. This is easier to do in high-trust churches than in low-trust
churches. Churches that are unclear about core values and bedrock beliefs, and vague about vision and mission, inevitably multiply bureaucracy.
Redundant levels of management end up revisiting and revising mission
team decisions because poor systems of accountability foment distrust.

High-trust churches reduce bureaucracy and allow teams freedom to innovate tactics to achieve measureable outcomes.

Strategic thinkers define broad strategies to achieve measureable outcomes, but they leave the tactical details to the teams. Therefore, strategic thinkers don't need to go into detail about when, how, or where ministry takes place. They only need to define specific boundaries within which any tactic can be innovated and developed.

When?

In our world, in which the pace of change is moving faster, time is the most valuable commodity of all. Timing is the most important tactical decision. Exactly when and how often will any given program or creative idea occur? How long will it continue? Exactly when will it be reevaluated, renewed, or ended? If the rationale and anticipated results are clear, then leaders should be clear about the public toward whom the program or ministry is targeted. There are many publics, but every single public is faced with innumerable competitive choices that claim part of their most valuable possession: time.

Timing is the first critical decision. Other tactical decisions will be made only in reference to this decision. In making decisions about timing, strategic thinkers must set aside all preconceived notions about "sacred" and "secular" time; or "private" and "public service" time; or "family" and "work-related" time. All time is potentially sacred. Any moment can be grasped by the Spirit to reveal eternal truth and the touch of the Holy. Segmented time has disappeared, and private or family time is blending into public service and work time.

Claims upon our time are now on a level playing field. Every claim competes with every other claim. You might say that every minute or second includes a balance of private, public service, family, and work-related components. You may be on holiday, but still available to the office; you may be at the office and still be text messaging your friends. You may enjoy a personal hobby, but part of the enjoyment will be the plan to use it for public service. You may do public service but use the opportunity for family enrichment.

Holistic time has replaced compartmentalized time. Life goes faster, people are multitasking, and God is revealed in even ordinary events. In that context, strategic thinkers need to know the following things about a project—and they don't need to know nearly anything else.

Start Time

This is the time when a team will take action. It may seem obvious that programs and creative ideas require a specific start time, but it is astonishing how often this is left vague or open ended. Such ambiguity alerts strategic thinkers to weaknesses in the proposal.

- This may reveal that the team isn't really serious about the urgency of the program's mission. If they keep postponing the start time to be convenient for their personal lifestyles or to fit in with the agendas of other groups or ministries, the importance of their own mission becomes questionable. If it is of God, then they will be expected to make sacrifices and be bold in asserting themselves for the mission.

- Ambiguity about start time may also reveal that the team is unclear about the public (demographic or lifestyle segment group) that they are trying to reach. The "right time" is always the "best time" for the mission target. That will be determined through research, focus groups, and other listening strategies. This is basic market research, which gives the mission team confidence for their initiative.

- Finally, ambiguity about start time may reveal that the team isn't intentional about training leaders and preparing resources to ensure success. The most common reason start times are delayed is that the team is "not ready." They aren't ready because team leaders haven't defined the standard of excellence carefully and haven't realistically equipped the team for action.

Therefore, the first thing strategic thinkers look for is a definitive start time for action. They might wonder if this is the best timing, and if so they will ask the team about it. The team should have a reasonable, well-researched answer.

Pattern of Activity

Schedules change, but there is usually a pattern for any activity. The pattern defines the regularity through which the team advances the mission. Of course, this varies according to the particular mission. This will also be customized for the public that is the mission target and will be determined through solid research. Patterns may change after evaluation and adjusted in response to feedback. Nevertheless, strategic thinkers must know the basic pattern of activity to ensure reasonable cooperation of all groups in the church. One team can't be allowed to block another mission team because each claims specific resources at the same time.

Patterns are always easier to identify for renewing programs than creative ideas. The threat for the team of any ongoing program is that the schedule is taken for granted. Strategic thinkers in the leadership summit may question the team to make sure the circumstances of the mission field haven't changed. The dilemma for the team implementing any creative idea is that the schedule is really a trial run. Strategic thinkers will be most insistent that an evaluation time is set.

Evaluation Time

The goal of evaluation is to determine if any given team is making concrete progress to achieve anticipated measurable results. If a team cannot, or will not, define anticipated measurable results, the program or creative idea shouldn't have gotten to the leadership summit in the first place.

Teams determine one or more evaluation times. The more carefully they have defined anticipated measurable results, the faster they can discern if they are being successful. The real work then begins.

- If the team is making progress toward anticipated measurable results, the ensuing conversation with strategic thinkers is all about making progress faster, with more relevance that will make personal or social change more likely to be permanent.

- If the team isn't making progress toward anticipated measurable results, the ensuing conversation is all about why and what they can do about it. This conversation connects directly to any ambiguities over

133

the start time. Aside from meddling and micromanagement by functional managers or the board in the church, failure to make progress is almost always due to the same three things. The team isn't urgent and sacrificial enough. The team isn't really sensitive to the mission field and the needs of the public they hope to reach. The team isn't sufficiently trained.

Depending on the program or creative idea, the strategic thinkers in the leadership summit may request an evaluation process. The team must have a clear method to gather the statistics, stories, or feedback that will measure success.

Closure Time

Every program or creative idea must state the time when the program or ministry will end. This is true even if the hope is that the program or ministry will be renewed and scheduled in the next year (or whenever the timetable for the project has run its course). This protects the church from entrenching sacred cow programs that may be dearly loved by some people but which have become largely irrelevant to advance the overall mission of the church. Closure means just that. It's over. It's time to return to God in prayer. If the Holy Spirit elicits the purpose, the leadership, and the measurable urgency from the hearts of the spiritually growing people *once again*, that is something to celebrate. But it may be that the program is finished or needs to be profoundly reinvented, and the only way to know that for sure is to stop, step back, and look.

Many programs outlive their relevance because the team members and the core group of people included in the ministry love each other too much. The mission has subtly shifted from outreach to strangers, to the preservation of harmony and mutual support of participants.

This will be clearly revealed when strategic thinkers force a team to anticipate closure. They are forced to restate the *why, who,* and *to what end* of the program. They have to revisit the original rationale for the program or creative idea; re-identify who really has the responsibility and authority to design, implement, and evaluate results; and redefine what the anticipated measurable results truly are.

This protects the church from a common, negative evolution that can occur in even the best programs and ministries. The hallmarks of this negative evolution are that leadership begins to rotate among volunteers and is not fixed to specifically called and trained leaders; the alignment between the program and the vision of the church becomes increasingly obscure; and the real measurement of success has more to do with the comfort and internal harmony of participants than actual personal or social change.

Many programs become entrenched in the budget and scheduling of the church, and unless the leaders *routinely* and *consistently* impose a closure time for every program and ministry, some teams will inevitably feel singled out for "persecution." Conflict will be inevitable. However, if the principle of closure is consistently applied, the process will become natural to the life of the church.

Clarity about start, pattern of activity, evaluation, and closure are the only essential things that strategic thinkers need to know about timing. All the other details can be entrusted to the ministry team. If the ministry team can't be trusted to fill in the details, then they aren't the right team to do it in the first place. Suddenly leaders realize that the program or creative idea shouldn't have made the first cut anyway, because they still don't know *who* will take authority and responsibility to do it.

Consider these examples of timing:

A healing worship service might be formally launched in September because many people put off medical surgeries, therapies, or counseling until after their vacations. This would allow worship and hospitality teams to be trained over the summer when volunteers might have more time. If the healing worship were located in Nashville or Birmingham, the best time slot might be Friday during the noon hour. This is because these cities have definable areas that concentrate medical facilities; people may drive a considerable distance to stay over a weekend to visit sick relatives; medical personnel are more likely to take lunch hour time at the end of the week for worship; and it would encourage patients who anticipate a lonely and depressing weekend stay. The evaluation time might be scheduled at the end of November and the end of March, which are transitional times for mental health, and include surveys for both patients and health care staff. The closure time may be two years hence, allowing plenty of opportunities for mission team leaders to make adjustments as they learn from experience.

A Bible study small group might be formally launched at the end of February to coincide with Lent. This would allow training and publicity to occur in the fall. If the Bible study were located in a rural environment, the best time slot might be Saturday morning or Sunday afternoon so that participants could drive in daylight and it wouldn't interrupt the work week. A survey of participants might follow the close of the Bible study after Easter to plan for the next year. If a group chooses to continue meeting as a small group after Easter, they would develop a new covenant defining the rationale, leadership, and anticipated measurable results; and rethink the tactics for scheduling.

A prayer chain might be formally launched on Pentecost Sunday, following a sermon series in the spring. Whether the prayer chain used e-mail, telephone, or personal conversations, the group would schedule every Wednesday evening for a small-group gathering in a private home to learn more about prayer, talk about emerging needs, and join hands for personal intercession. The schedule might also include a required e-mail from each member of the prayer chain to be sent to the pastor identifying the people for whom prayers were offered that week. The prayer chain would close the following May (one year) for re-evaluation.

A food bank might be formally launched on the first Monday in November because it was determined that the peak need for food in the community started with Thanksgiving, peaked with Christmas, and continued through the winter months. The food bank would be open every evening between 3:30 and 8:00 because this would allow single parents time to finish work, pick up children, and collect food before dark and children's bedtimes. Closure time would be set for the end of June. If the food bank was succeeding beyond expectation, the summer would be a convenient time to close temporarily and renovate or relocate.

Programs and creative ideas might be simpler or considerably more complex. However, the simplicity or complexity of the program or idea doesn't change the importance of concreteness about timing. Time is the most important resource today. All other tactics will be developed with this in mind. A mission team can have the best tactics in the world, but if the timing is wrong it will fail. Similarly, a mission team can succeed with modest standards of quality and resources if the timing is right.

How?

We come now to the part of strategic thinking for which many readers have been waiting patiently. Surely this is the real heart of the matter! Surely this is the most important aspect of planning! Now strategic thinkers in the leadership summit actually get to hear—and approve—the tactics of implementation.

You may be disappointed to realize that this is probably the least important step for the leadership summit. Strategic thinkers really don't care *how* a program or creative idea is implemented. They only care that it is aligned with the overall vision and mission of the church, that implementation stays within certain boundaries, and that the program or creative idea is extraordinarily successful. How that gets done is largely up to the mission team. Churches leaders have a great deal to do and can't micromanage everything. Just do it.

The real key here is "trust." The less often strategic thinkers *trust* mission teams, the more often they feel compelled to supervise implementation tactics and become strategic planners. The higher their trust, the more readily they distance themselves from those tactics. Do strategic thinkers really need to know? Do strategic thinkers have a reason to trust their mission teams? Church leaders with little real trust invest almost all of their time on micromanagement. They skip rapidly and superficially over everything else—dwell almost entirely on this—and then replace the rest of the planning process with what amounts to political negotiation.

Assuming that the leadership summit is truly about strategic thinking and not tactical negotiation, what do the summit participants really need to know about *how* a team will implement tactics? Perhaps the best way to understand this is to ask what the summit participants don't need to know.

Strategic thinkers don't need to know a great deal! They don't need to know how the healing worship mission team will advertise, how they will arrange the seating, or what kind of music they will use. They don't need to know what curriculum the Bible study mission team will choose or whether they will use video. They don't need to know how gender balanced the prayer chain will be or whether the prayer-chain mission team includes youth. They don't need to know whether the food bank mission team will offer sugar-free foods and name-brand products, or whether they will illuminate the room with fluorescent lighting. They do need to have reasonable assurance that all of these mission teams will never go beyond the boundaries of the core values, beliefs, vision, and mission of the church that is the consensus of the people—and they need to know that the teams have a good chance of being extraordinarily successful.

Therefore, there are three things about tactical implementation that strategic thinkers in the leadership summit do need to know.

First, strategic thinkers need to know how the team will train leaders. There should be a plan for basic training, problem solving, and ongoing coaching. Not only will this improve the mission alignment, integrity, skills and competencies, and teamwork of the volunteers in the mission team but it will replicate more leaders so that the program or creative idea can survive the potential burnout or rotation of its key leaders. How will the mission team acquire, train, evaluate, and (if necessary) dismiss volunteers? When will it happen? How will it happen? What resources will they use?

Strategic thinkers always assume that mistakes will be made. Indeed, they hope that mistakes will be made, because this reveals that a mission team is truly adapting and innovating for the changing mission field. Of course mistakes will be made! It's only by making mistakes that leaders learn new things. So the question for strategic thinkers is whether the team has anticipated this. Is there a plan for leadership development?

Second, strategic thinkers need to know what technologies will be required to fulfill the mission. I use the term *technologies* in the broadest sense. Digital tools are technologies. The planning team needs to know if the healing worship team will need special audio, video, or Internet technologies. However, any object or tool that allows a mission team to succeed is also "technology." Will the healing worship mission team require special seating, ramps for wheelchairs, pillows on the floor to catch people "slain in the Spirit," additional space for counseling, and so on?

The technology needs of a team will have fundraising and financial management implications. If a team only intends to *seed* new mission, the need for technology will inform the size of the grant. If the team intends to subsidize mission, the need for technology will inform the size of the stewardship campaign. Other concerns about technology may include issues of future property renovation and multipurpose space. If the healing worship mission team requires a unique floor plan and prayer stations, could that block the mission of some other worship team with a mission for inspirational concerts?

Third, strategic thinkers need to know what expertise will be required to fulfill the mission. This may or may not have implications for salaries since many faithful Christian professionals will offer their retirement or volunteer services for free. It is important to know if special certifications from the church or state will be necessary or if leaders will need specialized training from a community college or seminary. There may be legalities to observe, forms to fill out, liabilities to assume, or expectations to meet. The healing worship team may require specifically ordained or commissioned leaders to celebrate the sacraments of unction or communion. The food bank may require a part-time executive officer experienced in nonprofit operations. Even the prayer chain may require special accreditation from a mediation center or theological college.

Expertise might also take the form of consultancy. Mission teams might anticipate the need for an outside consultant to help develop strategic plans or equip volunteers. The food bank may need their volunteers to learn the basics of another language. The prayer chain might need to learn how to use e-mail, develop interactive websites, and use Internet voice communications. These are examples of time-limited contracts that might be deemed necessary for the success of the mission. Again, financial cost may or may not be a factor. The bigger issue may be the compatibility of outside consultants with the core values, beliefs, vision, and mission of the church itself.

That's really all there is to this step. Perhaps the hardest task for strategic thinkers is restraint. Once you ensure that any given team has a clear strategy for training, has identified whatever it needs for technologies, and has acquired whatever expertise might be necessary to do the work, move on.

Where?

The next question to answer is where implementation of the program or creative idea will take place. In a sense, this is a specific kind of technology, but it has much broader implications than many church leaders think. Paradoxically, even though church leaders invest considerable attention to the customization of sanctuary space, they are remarkably naïve about every other space. They think the program just needs a room with chairs in it or a building that doesn't leak. However, once strategic thinkers understand "when" and "how," the challenges of "where" become much clearer.

At one time the only two choices about location were church property (i.e., the primary church "campus" or "building") and other property owned or rented by the church. In the late 1990s, however, two things happened to radically change strategic thinking.

First, the Internet happened. The potential of cyberspace is to connect with the mobility and timidity of the public. People traveled or relocated as never before, and people became more timid about lasting, intimate relationships than ever before. This last change bears closer examination by leaders. For several decades we've seen increasing anxiety about intimate commitments. Not only have people divorced more often, and delayed marriage longer, they also require more inches of separation in the pew or in the fellowship hall. Larger rooms are needed to house the same number of people. The narthex in some places is transformed into a food court with multiple serving stations—even in some small churches. The sophistication of interactive websites allows increasingly timid publics even more power to "manage risk" in relationships and glimpse the Holy from a safe distance. Many people who will not enter a room will browse a website.

Second, the alienation of the public from the institutional church accelerated exponentially. A church can deploy the very best program, of high quality, incredibly useful and relevant to social and personal needs, *and people still won't come if it is located in the church.* The church building and "churchy" environments have become like a phobia for contemporary people. They just won't go there. They won't even enter a place associated with the ecclesiastical style of architecture. They can't stand to be around hymnbooks. They break out in spiritual hives if they come in contact with religious paraphernalia or sanctimonious people. This shift has encouraged a growing movement for multisite ministries. Churches literally locate programs or community groups far away from churchy environments so that spiritually hungry, institutionally alienated seekers will come.

Strategic thinkers should encourage teams to *literally* think "out of the box." Some programs and creative ideas might easily be implemented on church property. Perhaps the Bible study and prayer chain might meet in the parlor or library of the church each week—or perhaps not. These gatherings might better encourage youth, singles, or twentysomethings if the group met at the local coffee house. Perhaps the healing worship service might meet in the sanctuary, in a visually "holy" environment with the altar and baptismal font readily available—or perhaps not. The healing worship service might better be held in the multipurpose room of the medical center using paper cups for communion. Perhaps the food bank might operate from the basement of the church—but perhaps not. Perhaps hidden barriers of race, culture, language, or religion might be a hindrance. There are many who would rather go hungry than shame themselves by entering a church building.

The previous answers to the questions "when" and "how" will help strategic thinkers decide where to locate. These questions have forced leaders to consider the unique expectations of the public (demographic or lifestyle segment) they are trying to reach. Indeed, if there is no clarity about precisely *who* the program or ministry is designed to reach, it would never have survived the first cut.

The obvious question is whether the program or creative idea will be located on campus in the church building, at an offsite location, or in cyberspace. Which will be most effective to connect with the public the leaders want to reach? Always adjust the team to adapt for the target; never expect the target to adapt for the convenience or habits of the team. This seems obvious, but this mistake is made constantly because teams have hidden sacred cow assumptions that they bring to the planning process. They are apt to assume, for example, that all worship must happen in the traditional sanctuary or at a church building; all Bible study groups meet in a classroom; or all prayer chains will occur before or after work hours from a fixed residential telephone. Strategic thinkers insist that teams first understand the public who is the heartburst for mission. Then decide where to locate and design the space for mission.

There are three criteria for choosing the right place or the right space. Strategic thinkers should use these criteria as a template to assess any program or creative idea.

- *Environment:* An environment is the set of surrounding circumstances that encourage something to happen. These circumstances may be physical or symbolic. Physical circumstances include appropriate entrances and exits, lighting, heating or air conditioning, air quality, seating, safety and security equipment, and specialized equipment relevant to the purpose of the program. Symbolic circumstances include interior decorations, colors, images, textures, artifacts, and anything that creates a multisensory experience that communicates a special meaning or invokes a particular reaction.

- *Accessibility:* The public is increasingly sensitive to the elderly, the very young, pregnant mothers, and those with physical or mental limitations. They expect the church to at least equal the accessibility requirements of any public institution, and radical hospitality will drive the church to surpass the minimum. Ramps and elevators, wide doorways to main halls and rest rooms, hand grips for toilets, aisle access for walkers and wheelchairs, safe storage for the same, and technologies to assist people with limited hearing or eyesight are often required and certainly expected.

- *Quality Relationships:* One of the anticipated measurable results of any program or creative idea is that it will stimulate *conversation* between mentors and seekers. This is the most effective way for the church to draw people into a larger process of disciple making or simply to allow ministry leaders to interact with clients for their greater well-being. The conversation *may* take place away from the particular place and space of the ministry, but in our busy world there is no time like the present. A single word, pause for eye contact, or spontaneous conversation *right there* may have more significance than any future meeting, sermon, or study. Therefore, the best place and space will provide room for conversations to happen that will not block traffic, inhibit access, invade privacy, or compromise confidentiality.

Teams often overlook this important aspect of place and space. Strategic thinkers need to remind them that the church makes the sacrifices to bless the public, but the public should not make sacrifices for the convenience of the church. Even in cyberspace the choice of location must pay attention to the criteria of environment, accessibility, and quality relationships. This means that websites can no longer be static. They are virtual places and spaces where ministry happens for a definable, describable public. These virtual spaces must communicate Christian messages in a multisensory environment; be easily accessed with the fewest "clicks" and clearest directions; and include forums, blogs, chats, and other interactive methods for mentors and seekers to talk.

Where will the program or creative idea be located? The *place* will be on the church campus or in the church building; off site in an appropriate rented or owned location; or in cyberspace through a website, blog, forum, or other media. The *space* will be customized for environment, accessibility, and quality relationships.

Once again, let's revisit the planning process for St. Anonymous Church.

The recommendation of the worship team to the board and senior staff participants in the planning team was that the 11:00 a.m. worship service be radically changed. Instead of simply repeating the same educational-caregiving worship service that was celebrated at 9:30, it would be designed with a completely different focus, message, and leadership team. It would be extremely inspirational and more contemporary, and target lifestyle segments currently underrepresented in the church.

The idea was a surprise to the board in particular. They asked the worship team to participate in the discussion of this particular topic during the summit. When the team arrived, they began to lay out all the details related to *how* the new worship service would be designed. The board rightly interrupted to tell them that they didn't need to know that. And this was a surprise to the worship team.

You see, many members of the worship team had only experienced low-trust churches. Therefore, they came to the summit already defensive about their proposal. They assumed the meeting would be a political negotiation, as board members claiming to "represent" various factions in the church complained about tactics that were outside their comfort zones. At St. Anonymous, this didn't happen. The board was more concerned about achieving God's mission to bless strangers to grace than about their comfort zones.

The conversation of the leadership summit got back on track. It was occasionally stressful but for different reasons.

First, the worship team explained *when* the revamped worship service would occur. It would start in September when the younger singles and young families were back from vacations and summer self-time, and returning to disciplines of work and education. The more stressful issues over timing were these:

- It would still be at 11:00 Sunday morning since the people in the target lifestyle segments either overslept after Saturday night fun or had young children who required more time to get ready for church. This would mean that the prime time on Sunday morning would *not* be set aside for current members.

- It would only be evaluated after eighteen months. The targeted lifestyle segments tended to be undisciplined about church attendance, and it would take that long to discern whether or not this new worship service would become a priority in their schedules. This meant that significant resources of the church would be committed for a new venture.

Assuming that the initiative was successful, the potential closing time for the service would be three years away—at the time of the next leadership summit.

The strategic thinkers in the leadership summit only needed to know three essential things about *how* the revamped worship service would be designed. The ministry team explained—and again raised stress levels.

- The new worship leadership would require training. The band would need to be enhanced with new musicians, or the current musicians would need some additional coaching. The senior pastor would also need extra training to shift from being a purely expository preacher to a motivational speaker.

- In order for the new inspirational worship service to have a big sound, the audio systems would need to be upgraded, and the electrical supply to the old building would need to be improved or replaced.

The team did not think that they would need to hire a consultant, but they did think it would be helpful to send worship leaders to see and experience inspirational worship services in other churches.

Finally, the worship team elaborated on the location and design of the facility (i.e., *where* the worship service would occur). They were convinced that the current sanctuary would be suitable, since the beauty of the architecture and symbolism of the stained-glass windows would enhance the inspirational experience. Two things would need to be changed:

- The church would need to remove the last few rows of pews in the back of the sanctuary. This would make space for more comfortable chairs and a few infant strollers, which would be more inviting to timid seekers.

- The church would need to create a second hospitality center on the same level as, and immediately proximate to, the sanctuary. This would be more likely to encourage the singles and couples in these busy lifestyle segments to linger longer.

Both these changes would be "costly" in more ways than one, but they would enhance the relational aspects of the space that would be crucial to success in reaching these people.

Strategic thinkers in the leadership summit must be convinced that the rationale for any initiative (why, who, and anticipated results) is clearly in line with organizational identity and organizational success. That's the first cut for the agenda of the leadership summit. They also must be sure that all teams (staff and volunteers) know the basic boundaries within which to innovate all tactics. This becomes the second cut for the leadership summit. Even if a program or idea is aligned with organizational identity and success, no program or idea should be considered further if the basic boundaries for action are unclear. Once the list of programs and ideas for innovation and implementation by teams is clear, the really hard work begins!

Perspiration

The Cost

As I said at the beginning of this chapter, there are two basic goals for a leadership summit. The first is to set priorities. The board defines the broad strategies to achieve results that align with vision, and trusts the tactics to teams. The second outcome of a summit, however, is to calculate the true cost of discipleship and anticipate the stress of change. The teams have authority and responsibility to innovate and implement whatever tactics will achieve the desired results. They don't need to assume the added burden of conflict resolution or stress management that change inevitably brings.

The goal of the leadership summit isn't to preserve harmony at any cost but to define and address the sacrifices the church must make in order to be faithful to God's mission. You often hear church people—and disgruntled church people in particular—say that *the church should be run like a business.* Superficially they are correct. Money matters. It shouldn't be spent on pet projects or to satisfy personal preferences, but it should be spent to maximize the *acceleration* and *impact* of the church itself. The profound error in this statement, however, is the assumption that the church is a typical organization that is mainly concerned with the costs of *preservation* and *production*, and that the outputs of the church are *programs* and *charitable contributions*. That is incorrect. The church is in fact about as atypical an organization as you can find. It is mainly concerned with the *costs of discipleship*, and the principle outputs of the church will be *more disciples* and a transformed world that is closer to *the realm of God*.

I've written several times about the difference between the approach to planning by high-trust churches and low-trust churches. This is most apparent in the way they manage risk and meet the cost of discipleship.

Strategic *thinking* is what high-trust churches do. High-trust churches spend a great deal of energy building and embedding a consensus of core values and bedrock beliefs, and clarity about motivating vision and measureable mission. They never even spend energy planning a program for which the rationale, leadership, and outcomes are unclear. They resist micromanagement and focus on tactical essentials. And when it comes to counting the cost of change they always *start* with the cost of changing attitudes and work their way down through the next five cost centers, discussing the financial cost last of all. This is why strategic thinking for these boards and ministry teams isn't a burden but an exciting adventure.

Low-trust churches are foggy about values and beliefs, vision and mission. And in a fog, they empower "foghorns" to control any planning. These are influential personalities who superimpose their own priorities, tastes, value systems, and theological and ideological perspectives on the life and work of the church. Of necessity, they *must* micromanage, and since there is usually more than one "foghorn faction" in the church every strategic decision becomes a political negotiation. They always focus on money because it is the root of power. The chronic complaint about being poor is a way to camouflage the *real* costs of attitude and tradition, organization and leadership, and technology and property that they are unwilling to pay (and often unwilling to admit). This is why strategic planning for these boards and committees is a burden best avoided.

Strategic *planning* is what low-trust churches do. A low-trust church must really trust the elected officers or appointed leaders. Note that trust here isn't a universally understood and consistently applied consensus for core values and bedrock beliefs. It is simply confidence that duly nominated, elected, or appointed institutional officers will protect the traditions, polities, privileges, and processes of the institution. Trust them. Trust the method through which they were chosen. These churches will spend enormous energy shaping, solidifying, and communicating these institutional processes.

That *might* work. Increasingly, however, trust in the institutional system is breaking down. It isn't that such trust is *never* deserved but that too often it is *not* deserved, and that is enough to introduce a skepticism that pervades the entire planning process. The machinations of the "system" don't seem to match, reveal, or even promote the core values, beliefs, vision, and mission that are a consensus. Indeed, the "system" is all there is, and there really is no consensus.

All committees aspiring to use the resources of the church to implement programs and creative ideas are suddenly faced with uncertainty. They set out to do ministry and mission, but they end up playing politics. They want to be disciples, but suddenly they are treated as fundraisers. They want to bless the world in the name of Christ, but they are told the church can't afford the programs. This is why traditional Christendom churches have trouble thinking strategically. They tend to ignore the point of mission and sustain the status quo. They tend to micromanage tactics and get preoccupied about costs. Strategic thinking is reduced to strategic planning and subverted by politics.

In a typical business or nonprofit, cost is always measured in money. In the typical church, there are in fact seven distinct cost centers:

- the cost of changing local and organizational traditions;
- the cost of changing personal and membership attitudes;
- the cost of adapting leadership expectations;
- the cost of adapting organizational structures;
- the cost of acquiring and renovating properties;
- the cost of upgrading and learning technologies;
- the cost of financial support.

In North America, at least, churches that are willing to pay the cost of discipleship by changing attitudes and traditions, adapting organization and leadership, and upgrading technologies and properties *will always find the money*. There are very few places in North America, even in some of the remotest areas and poorest neighborhoods, in which *money by itself* is ever the real obstacle to relevant ministry.

How much is the cost? Think of the cost of discipleship not just as a single, financial cost but as a series of overlapping cost centers. This is most faithful to the teaching of Jesus and the history of the earliest church.

Financial cost is clearly important in the Gospels and Epistles, but is always a secondary matter tied to other costs. The financial cost for the "rich young ruler" may be to sell all he has and give to the poor, but he can only pay that cost if he is already prepared to pay the cost in clarifying faith and changing lifestyle. Ananias and Sapphira may be punished for failing to pay the financial cost but only because they failed to pay the deeper cost of obedience and compassion.

Strategic thinkers define the cost of discipleship for any given program or creative idea in successive steps. This is particularly important when a church is considering major changes like church mergers, major capital campaigns, and signature outreach ministries (or nonprofits).[9] But it is also important for seemingly small changes, minor adjustments, and new initiatives. All too often what seems small in the summit looms large in the wider congregation.

Cost in Changing Tradition

The first—and often most painful—cost center is about changing tradition. This is usually about local or congregational tradition.

The answers to the questions of *when* or *where* create anxiety because the church must alter or replace sacred times or sacred objects. The Sunday morning schedule must change, even though it has worked well for decades. A room must be renovated even though a memorial window or other object has to be relocated or the classic architecture must be changed. A projection screen must be installed, even though it occasionally will cover the organ pipes. The unused chapel must be dismantled to create education space, even though it was dedicated in memory of a dearly loved former pastor and is on picture postcards. A building must be demolished even though it is precious to the community historical society.

The answer to the question of *how* creates anxiety because the church must alter its behavioral habits. People will say, "We've never done it this way before." The program or creative idea may require different liturgical

---

9. Coauthor Page Brooks and I write about this extensively in *Church Mergers* (Lanham, MD: Rowan and Littlefield, 2016).

patterns, musical instrumentations, styles, or languages. The small group may use curricula published by different agents; the prayer chain may use different media; or the food bank may distribute different products. The program or idea takes church members beyond the comfort zones of familiar habits.

Anxious people will often argue that proposed changes contradict *denominational* church practices. This is actually rare and limited to changes that impact clear sacramental practices of the church. The reality is that all denominations began as "original innovators." They were all mavericks from past traditions and known for their remarkable experimentation and openness to new ideas and techniques. Many nineteenth- and early twentieth-century "traditions" that we attribute to essential denominational life are in fact just pragmatic decisions that have become self-perpetuating. The "traditions" of Salvation Army uniforms, brass bands, and Christmas collections, for example, are no more sacred than any tactic. The innovation of William Booth was to start with a blank page and simply borrow from the best and most effective military, corporate, and social service organizations of his day in order to do whatever it took to accomplish God's mission.

It is the clarity of vision and mission that will always inform strategic thinkers when they evaluate this first cost center for discipleship. The more clearly they focus the mission and vision of the church, the better they can test the alignment of any program or idea to that mission. They will be less prone to diversion in order to protect some local tradition.

Cost in Changing Attitude

The second cost center that must be considered by strategic thinkers in the implementation of any idea or program is what price will be required to change attitudes. There are two layers to this cost center: corporate and personal.

Some bad attitudes are unconsciously shared by everyone in the church. They can be described as *corporate addictions*, or self-destructive habits that organizations chronically deny. These addictions need to be uncovered and corrected for positive change to occur.

A common example is the attitude of "membership privilege." The inclination to "me first" comes as naturally to established church members as it does to average American citizens. The attitude of membership privilege builds even in the best and most intentional churches. Members work hard as volunteers, and wise leaders always affirm or reward their efforts. The expectation of reward tends to be proportionate to the labor of the volunteer. Surely those who work hardest should receive the firstfruits of their labors! And surely the members who pay for the church should receive institutional benefits! It is difficult for hardworking volunteers to hear the hard words of Jesus that *the first must be last, and the last must be first.*

Corporate addiction tends to be revealed in the daily and weekly behavior of church members, but it may be even more painfully revealed on Sunday mornings and on special occasions. The *members* don't see it. But *visitors* see it right away, and it discourages participation in the church. Visitors see that the music of worship honors the tastes of the members. The refreshments respect the culture of the members. The weddings at the church are free only for the members. On Christmas Eve, when visitors are most likely to attend worship, visitors may be ignored as members gather in their own families and friendship circles.

Other bad attitudes are revealed by the prejudice of individuals and their factions. These are usually unconscious prejudices that undermine or contradict the core values shared by the church. Despite what the church says, individual members reveal prejudices over race, gender, age, handicap, and sexuality. Other prejudices include ethnicity, language, and country of origin; marital status, child-rearing, and dual careers; or income, occupation, and even housing.

Prejudice today is more likely to be expressed between lifestyle segments. There are some lifestyle segments that are compatible with other lifestyle segments but suspicious of, or hostile toward, other lifestyle segments. You can often anticipate this by studying a theme map of lifestyle segmentation in your community or mission field.

For example, some lifestyle segments such as "Silver Sophisticates" (C13) often live near "American Royalty" (A01) with whom they are quite compatible, but intentionally distance themselves from "Digital Dependents" (O51). On the other hand, the lifestyle segments of Group O "Striving Singles" often mingle with the baby boomers of "Boomers and Boomerangs" (C14) and "Rooted Flower Power" (L42). Incompatible lifestyle segments may not intentionally denigrate other lifestyle segments, but often they subtly stereotype and mock one another in humorous (but hurtful) ways.

Strategic thinkers always look at the church through the eyes of visitors, seekers, strangers, and marginalized people. It isn't the scripted sermon or strategic plan that reveals the truth about congregational attitudes but the unrehearsed word and spontaneous deed.

It's the clarity of core values and bedrock beliefs that will always inform strategic thinkers when they evaluate this second cost center for discipleship. The more clearly core values and beliefs are understood, and the more rigorously they are used as a primary vehicle for accountability for all leaders and members, the better they can test the alignment of any program or idea to that mission. Strategic thinkers will be less likely to excuse bad attitudes and much bolder to reveal and change them.

Cost in Changing Leadership

The priority for strategic thinkers isn't to protect jobs but to succeed as an organization. Paid or unpaid leaders may need to be hired (acquired) or fired (dismissed) in order to redeploy the leadership assets of the church. Certain leadership positions may become redundant as programs change and creative ideas emerge, or they may simply be reduced in significance and the portfolio may need to be downsized. Other leadership positions may become urgent. Gaps need to be filled, or the leadership portfolio needs to be expanded.

When the goal of strategic thinking is organizational success rather than job protection, job descriptions are written (or rewritten) in a new way. In the past, job descriptions were long lists of tasks to be performed. Today job descriptions define the mission, clarify boundaries for creativity, and define measureable outcomes. In other words, strategic thinkers expect staff and volunteer leaders to *also* be strategic thinkers. They don't simply wait to be told what to do. They only need to know what they may *not* do, and they are expected to innovate tactics to get results.

This expectation can be terrifying to traditional church leaders. Some leaders, for example, only understand their ministry as a task to do certain work rather than as a calling to achieve certain results. Staff may want authority to do certain tactics but avoid responsibility for achieving outcomes that grow the church and change the world. Volunteers may want responsibility to do certain tactics but avoid authority to creatively adapt ministries in a changing world.

The cost of changing leadership isn't merely about function. It is also about identity. Credibility is more important today than function. The success of any program or creative idea often depends more on the ability of leaders to be role models, storytellers, and spiritual guides for the staff or volunteers who make up their team. They cannot be merely professionals. They must be truly Christians. And they must be able to mentor others as they seek to model values, articulate beliefs, and strive for mission.[10]

There is a protocol to ensure fair treatment for both staff and volunteers. Leaders should have options for additional training or mentoring. They should be given a reasonable amount of time to acquire new skills or adapt themselves to changing ministry demands. The first option may be to redeploy leaders for ministry who better use their gifts and talents. Strategic thinkers understand that you can't fire or dismiss a leader who isn't routinely evaluated; you can't evaluate a leader who isn't trained; and you can't train a leader who isn't clear about the mission, boundaries, and outcomes of their work in the first place.

Strategic thinkers may need to make hard choices. This doesn't mean that they are uncaring. It only means that they must be faithful.

- One thing strategic thinkers must not do is leave an ineffective leader, who can't or won't change, in the same leadership position. Ineffective leaders become organizational liabilities that decelerate church growth and reduce mission impact. Dysfunctional leaders become the mission itself rather than the agents of mission. Leadership change is not about politics but purposefulness.

---

10. See my book *Spiritual Leadership: Why Leaders Lead and Why People Follow* (Nashville: Abingdon Press, 2016).

- One thing strategic thinkers must avoid is hiring or appointing the wrong leader simply to fill a gap or implement a program. No matter how urgent a ministry seems to be, it is always better to wait, pray, and search for the right leader than fill a vacuum with the wrong person. The program will inevitably struggle or fail, and it is less stressful (and more compassionate) to wait than hire and the fire the wrong person.

Strategic thinkers understand that things are always changing, and leaders must always be growing. As the leader goes, so goes the program. As the leader grows, so grows the program.

Cost in Changing Organization

Organizations are defined by policy and practice. There are specific policies that extend core value, beliefs, vision, and mission to define organizational ends, procedures, and limitations on authority. There are specific practices for education, communication, and action. None of this is carved in stone. Organizations are organic. Organizations adjust and adapt as the mission expands. Policies will be revised. Practices will be changed.[11]

We often hear church members say that leaders were "forced" to change policies to comply with changing cultural mores or government regulations. More often than not, however, strategic thinkers were not "forced" to change. They seized opportunities by changing. New government regulations about fire and security actually created opportunities to upgrade kitchens to expand ministry to the homeless and protect children from abuse in Sunday school or nursery. New denominational policies about marriage or the celebration of the Eucharist actually created opportunities to reach out to a more diverse public. Members might chafe, but church growth accelerated and mission impact expanded.

Strategic thinkers change congregational policies for much the same reasons. The lines of communication and accountability may need to change in order to develop an innovative ministry. Practices for fund-

---

11. See my book *Spirited Leadership: Empowering People to Do What Matters* (Atlanta: Chalice Press, 2006).

raising and policies for financial management may need to change to raise more capital and disburse investments more flexibly. Requirements for worship or program leadership may need to change in order to include different age groups, open opportunities for women, or protect basic human rights.

Rigid bureaucracies block change. Fluid or organic organizations readily adapt to changing circumstances. They can quickly seize opportunities, correct problems, and customize programs. They can readily shift priorities or reshape committees and teams. Yet organizational stress also causes stress.

The more successful an organization becomes, the more pressure there will be to streamline structure. The process is akin to pruning a tree. Some committees, task groups, offices, or teams must be terminated so that other mission units grow. If the tree isn't pruned there will eventually be a tangle of branches that stunt the growth of the whole organism. If the structure isn't streamlined, bureaucracy will slow down decision-making time and stretch resources, reducing the productivity of the organization.

The problem is that committees and ministry teams often become "congregations" within the "congregation." Their ultimate allegiance is to the committee rather than the church, and they resist any attempt to redeploy, retrain, downsize, or diversify. This is particularly problematic for churches that don't have an intentional mentoring process that helps volunteers move from one group to another for their next step in spiritual growth. The longer individuals remain with the same people, the more their personal development slows down. Figuratively speaking, committees "love one another to death."

Many churches are often better known for their method of governance than their actual beliefs. Structure itself is considered sacred. Changes to structure therefore require biblical rationales, historical precedents, or the approval of episcopal leaders or denominational courts. More is at stake here than just tradition. The more strategic thinkers treat every practice and policy as "mere tactics," and the more they freely delegate authority and responsibility to teams, the harder it is for denominational hierarchies to control change.

Strategic thinkers understand that power is no longer simply exercised through the control of structure. It is exercised through the credibility of leaders and teams, and through the pragmatism of what works or doesn't work for church growth and mission impact.

Cost in Changing Property

Changes in attitude, leadership, and organization are often precipitated by changes in property or technology. Sometimes it is obvious what changes will be stressful. Properties and technologies in the past have been purchased and installed as memorial gifts. Change might actually require the legal permission of a family to repurpose, relocate, sell, or even destroy memorials. Often it isn't obvious. The smallest object can have enormous emotional import for individuals or families. Change might require intentional or extensive diplomacy to avoid factions and fighting.

It is common to hear church developers (especially *Protestant* church developers) say that there is no such thing as "sacred property." They say that there are only "sacred purposes." This distinction really isn't accurate. In Catholic, Anglican, and Orthodox traditions there really can be something sacred about properties or physical objects. Although Protestants are loath to admit it, the intuition that certain things are especially holy is built into the human experience. And it lingers in Protestant churches as well.

Property (e.g., architecture, facilities, and even landscaping) has symbolic power. Certain "things" seem more transparent to God than other things. A flower garden or a memorial wall to veterans carries more spiritual import than a parking lot or a playground. Similarly, the chancel and chapel indoors are more spiritually significant than carpeting and heating ducts. Therefore, the cost of changing property, at its most profound level, is the cost of changing *symbols*. The symbolic power of properties or objects can shift to other properties and objects, but sometimes this requires a deliberate act of worship or a continuous discipline of prayer before it can be accomplished. Everything is changeable, but that doesn't mean that all things are of equal value or significance.

Once again, clarity about the core values and bedrock beliefs of the church, and discernment about God's vision for the church are crucially important. This cost center is huge for those churches with vague values and beliefs and generic visions. These are churches with a corporate culture of low accountability. This transforms even the smallest changes to property and technology into major debates and slow decision making. Churches with greater clarity and alignment, with a culture of universal and consistent accountability, make changes more easily and quickly.

Some property change will be dramatic. The church may need to build a new worship center, education wing, or recreation area; it may need to build a second campus several miles away; or it may need to acquire a specialized building for some signature outreach ministry in residential housing, medical treatment, and so on. Some change will be relatively superficial. The church may need to remove pews, renovate classrooms and restrooms, or add serving stations. The church may need to relocate the main church building, rent temporary space, or even merge property assets with another church.

Other property changes will be seemingly invisible, but this doesn't mean that there will be no cost. Transplanting a tree, paving a parking lot, or renovating a classroom may go unnoticed by most members and visitors—unless they significantly change the sacred "ambience" of indoor or outdoor space. Church members sense that the property "feels different." Seekers may initially be attracted to a church more because of the symbolism of architecture, historicity of objects, or feeling of serenity that exists. And they may be discouraged from church participation when that changes.

Strategic thinkers find ways to honor sacred space or sacred objects, even as they renovate rooms and introduce contemporary symbols. The first step is to understand how sacred space and sacred objects are only sacred insofar as they are transparent to the Holy. They not only *remind* of God but they become portals through which humans can experience the touch and feel the breath of God. The second step is to explain how different lifestyle segments respond to different symbols as sacred and that God can use literally space or objects to remind and reveal divine grace.

Cost in Upgrading Technology

All facilities are a form of technology, but it is helpful to separate technology into a separate cost center for change. Property is primarily about symbolism. Technology is primarily about learning methodology. People learn in different ways. In the middle ages, when most people were illiterate, learning occurred through the technologies of stained glass, vestments, and the drama of worship. In the nineteenth century, when most people were literate, learning occurred through the technologies of the written and spoken word. And in the postmodern world of the new millennium, people tend to learn best from still and moving images, music, and animation. Long distance and interactive education is forcing churches to develop websites, podcasts, blogs, chat rooms, and social media presence.

The cost center for technology doesn't emphasize what is holy but what is effective. Technological change is really all about upgrading, updating, and focusing the best learning methodologies. Perhaps there can be something profoundly sacred about chalice and paten, but there is really nothing sacred about print. A computer is just a tool. We use it instead of a typewriter because it is faster, easier, more adaptable, and better at integrating word and image.

When a church fails to upgrade technology, it is a general admission that communication and learning are no longer top priorities. And indeed, these are *not* priorities in many churches. Learning threatens dogmatisms. Learning redistributes power. Learning invites dialogue and questions blind obedience. Technological change is stressful because it involves a power struggle between the old and the young, between the professionals and the amateurs, or between the "haves" and the "have nots." The real cost of installing video screens in the sanctuary, for example, is that it threatens the influence of one group and increases the influence of another.

The cost of technological change has little to do with financial cost. The expense of installing video screens and providing Internet access in the sanctuary is far less than the cost to upgrade kitchens to meet municipal codes or to fix heating and air conditioning. Yet the first change can provoke fistfights on the front lawn of the church, while the other changes simply challenge the annual stewardship campaign. Some changes seem small and are huge; other changes seem huge but are small.

Strategic thinkers understand that in countless ways the media really is the message. That is, the credibility and relevance of an organization is revealed first by its methodologies. It is only when the methodology is embraced that the message can be heard. If the methodology is dated or ineffective, people won't wait to hear the message. This seems to contradict traditional institutional assumptions. The church assumed that the Christian message should be effective in and of itself, regardless of how it is communicated. Today the attention span of people is so short, and technologies are changing so fast, that churches must upgrade and adapt technology just to get a hearing in the babble of competing markets.

Cost in Financial Investment

The last cost center is financial. It is important, but it is not the most important cost center. It is certainly true that every church has limited financial resources, but the limitations on those financial resources have more to do with perceived traditions, attitudes, leadership readiness, organizational openness, and clarity of mission. It is rarely true in North America that "churches don't have money." Most often it is true that churches aren't prepared to sacrifice enough to raise it, nor are they motivated enough to spend it.

Some of the cost for financial investment lies in the expertise, advice, and guidance churches provide mission teams to apply for grants, seek out partners, and network across sectors to accomplish more mission than they can afford alone. Charitable giving in America has been growing exponentially since 1965, and, except for a brief plateau in 2001, it has been growing consistently since. Mission teams are learning how to connect with other agencies and partners to finance mission.

Some of the cost for financial investment lies in the expertise, coordination, and guidance churches acquire through capital campaign professionals and stewardship consultants. Fund-raising is more complicated and beyond the capacity of most amateur church leaders today. With consulting help, mission teams and congregations always increase giving to the church beyond what they could accomplish themselves (even including the fee paid to the fund-raiser).

Some of the cost for financial investment lies in the promotion of designated giving. Most people prefer designated giving so that they can be assured that their contributions go to the mission targets closest to their hearts with the least overhead. However, the price of designated giving is that less popular or more controversial missions have a harder time competing for the attention of givers. This is why most denominations prefer unified budgets.

Finally, some of the cost of financial investment lies in the division of the limited resources available. Team-based churches that "seed" programs and creative ideas with specific investments from their capital pools must determine how many ministries can be adequately seeded and supported to raise additional funds. Hierarchical churches that "subsidize" programs and creative ideas from unified budgets have a greater challenge deciding which programs will not be funded at all.

Ultimately, however, money means power. Power means competition. Competition brings stress. Strategic thinkers realize that this is, in fact, a *good* thing.

1. Teams are encouraged to work together. Financial challenge breaks them out of their fixation on specific kinds of work ("program silos") and forces them to see the bigger picture of ministry. More than any other cost center, the financial challenge encourages team building.

2. The financial challenge also nudges teams toward entrepreneurship. The general budget should *never* subsidize the entire ministry. The assumption that the institution should pay for everything actually discourages radical generosity. This is why

growing churches develop mission-driven budgets that exceed inflationary increases. Teams are forced to be creative, and partially rely on designated giving.

3. Teams are forced to test popular support. In recent years, denominations and seminaries have expected churches to prioritize unpopular causes. Theoretically, this encourages "prophetic" thinking that challenges the status quo. In practice, this encourages top-down control that is often at odds with bottom-up mission. And in post-Christendom, the Holy Spirit is more likely to speak through the heartburst from below rather than the brainstorm from above.

Strategic thinkers understand that competition only becomes a *bad* thing when it devolves into confrontation. However, experience has shown that if churches are ready to pay the cost of discipleship by changing tradition, attitude, leadership, organization, property, and technology, then the financial cost rarely blocks strategic thinking.

The Stress

The second part of this stage in strategic thinking that I call "perspiration" is stress management. Strategic thinkers should not only discern priorities but also anticipate stress. Stress will be inevitable, but it can be minimized and managed to energize rather than deflate and accelerate instead of slow down.

The source of all stress management is the clarity and consensus of the organization about the foundation of trust (core values and bedrock beliefs), and the alignment of all people and programs of the organization to energizing purpose (motivating vision and mission outcomes). When the Heart Beat and Heart Song are clear, consistent, and universal as the primary vehicle of accountability, the *more stress* the church can endure, the more daring church leaders can be. When this congregational DNA is foggy and used only inconsistently and selectively, the *less stress* the church can endure, and the more likely the church will experience conflict over changing programs and creative ideas.

Strategic thinkers can use demographic, psychographic, and lifestyle research to anticipate stress. This is one major reason that churches should complete their People Plot on the MissionInsite search engine. They can download a ComparativeInsite Report that can indicate compatibility and incompatibility among groups *within* the church and *between* the church and the community. Different lifestyle segments have different expectations for ministry. Any change that helps a church bless lifestyle segments underrepresented in the church will inevitably cause stress among those lifestyle segments overrepresented in the church.

Strategic thinkers address the stress around changing traditions and attitudes by encouraging *personal growth*. After all, it is the self-satisfaction and contentment of members and majorities that keeps ministries from adapting to bless seekers and minorities. Established churches today have incredibly small commitments to personal growth and therefore struggle to change corporate addictions and personal habits. This is in stark contrast to the priorities of most of those churches in previous centuries. Adult faith formation and intentional spiritual growth were once extraordinarily important to the church. Adult classes and study groups multiplied and interfaced with strong teaching from the pulpit. Not surprisingly, the churches in previous centuries were remarkably adaptive to the changing cultures of the American frontier, the cultural diversity in other continents, and the seismic changes around the world.

MissionInsite can help you understand the different worldviews and hidden assumptions among different groups of people. When an individual or group likes or dislikes any change, you can go to the root of the matter to discover *why*. Moreover, you can recognize their different learning methodologies in education or small groups to customize an effective process for education and discernment.

Strategic thinkers address the stress of changing leadership and organization by requiring *team accountability*. We already know that consistent and universal accountability for values, beliefs, and alignment to vision reduces confrontation and increases healthy competition that encourages teamwork, creativity, and sensitivity. But there must also be consistent and universal accountability among paid and unpaid leaders (staff or committees) to policies of the church. There are three kinds of policies:

1. "Ends policies" are really measureable outcomes. When leaders are routinely held accountable to achieve the goals of *the body*, and not just goals of personal biases or committee agendas, the stress of change is greatly reduced. Change is no longer subjective and a battle of wills but objective, making adjustments to achieve common goals.

2. "Process policies" are really decision-making habits. When leaders are routinely held accountable to develop plans and implement tactics based on common assumptions, clear procedures, and relevant channels of collaboration, the stress of change is greatly reduced. Change is no longer the product of individual brainstorms and personal intimidation but is the result of a common method of discernment and communication.

3. "Executive limitations" are really specific prohibited actions. Although this sounds negative, it is really positive. When leaders are held accountable to stay within specific boundaries to protect safety and confidentiality, coordinate action, and learn specific things, the stress of change is greatly reduced. Leaders are encouraged to take initiative, provided they avoid doing certain dangerous or ineffective things that compromise integrity and sidetrack mission.

Accountability to policy is embedded into the culture of an organization when churches are diligent to hire staff or acquire volunteers; train staff or volunteer committees; regularly evaluate success; and fire staff, dismiss volunteers, or dissolve committees who are unable or unwilling to follow policy after a reasonable period of coaching or counseling.

MissionInsite can help you develop a culture of accountability with the tools of demographic, psychographic, and lifestyle research. A church needs to identify measureable outcomes, and research can help you understand exactly what you should measure. A church needs to standardize certain methods of decision making, and research can help you understand how different groups of people think and what choices they are likely to make. A church needs to protect the safety, integrity, effectiveness, and teamwork of the organization, and research can help you know how different groups experience vulnerability, define credibility, respond positively, and collaborate willingly.

Strategic thinkers address the stress of changing property and technology by encouraging *mission sensitivity*. Earlier we saw that property and technology aren't merely about things. Property is about symbols that are pregnant with meaning. Technology is about methods to learn and share ideas and hopes. Different lifestyle segments gravitate to different kinds of symbol systems and communication techniques. The Holy is transparent in different ways to different people. Some are moved by ecclesiastical architectures and traditional Christendom symbols, communicate best through print and corded telephones, and experience intimacy only in face-to-face gatherings. Others are moved by utilitarian or modern architectures and contemporary, natural, or abstract symbols. They communicate best through the Internet and smart phones, and they experience intimacy through social media. This doesn't make one group any better than another. They are just different. And they all deserve respect.

Strategic thinkers address the stress of changing financial investment by coaching members to make *lifestyle adjustments*. Stewardship isn't limited because of a lack of money. It's limited because church members aren't disciplined or intentional about their generosity. Church members are unwilling to make lifestyle adjustments in housing, transportation, food consumption, leisure time, and other personal preferences in order to increase financial giving to the church and God's mission. If these lifestyle adjustments are not modeled by paid and unpaid church leaders, the members won't risk their own stability or comfort zones very much.

A generous gift isn't the same as a generous life. The conversation about tithing isn't about giving a tenth to God but about giving everything to God and living on a tenth. Lifestyle adjustment is a huge challenge for consumer cultures. If the church only does fundraising, then people will always think they are poor. If the church coaches faithful household financial planning, then people will realize they are richer than they think.

Once again, MissionInsite can help you address this stress. You can do specific research about giving patterns in the community or download specific reports.

- ExecutiveInsite Reports provide data about occupation and income. You can compare your community to state averages. That helps you understand what kind of households and household wealth are in the mission field, and you can adapt coaching for faithful household financial planning to be basic or more advanced. You can anticipate the kind of charitable giving and diversity of financial investment relevant for households in the community and provide the right information in the right way. You can benchmark charitable giving in the community to different charities (including the church) and compare that to benchmarks in church giving.

- ComparativeInsite Reports provide data about the real financial potential within the church in contrast to the community. You can see the financial potential for each lifestyle segment in the community. You can study proportionate lifestyle representation in the church and estimate the real financial potential with church membership. The result is usually surprisingly high. You can then demonstrate how the financial potential of the church can be tapped if members were motivated to increase giving by only a few percent.

MissionInsite helps you overcome the pretense of poverty and determine the real wealth among church members. This allows you to set realistic capital campaign targets and identify realistic annual budget increases.

Strategic thinkers realize that there is a price to be paid for changing programs and empowering creative ideas. That price is an investment in the future of the church. The real "wealth" of a church doesn't come from their certified deposits or reserve funds but from the passion for personal growth, readiness for leadership accountability, sensitivity to the changing mission field, and courage to make lifestyle adjustments for the sake of God's mission. It is from that reserve of wealth that the church will pay the price of mission.

Strategic thinking always generates stress. The only way to eliminate stress entirely would be to remove any expectations for personal growth, leadership accountability, mission sensitivity, or lifestyle adjustment. In other words, the only way to eliminate stress is to avoid strategic thinking altogether (which, unfortunately, is what many churches actually do).

Strategic thinkers know that stress is inevitable. The real question is how much stress can be tolerated by the organization. As I said earlier, the degree of stress tolerated by any organization exactly corresponds to the universality and consistency of accountability to shared values, beliefs, vision, and mission. However, the faster and further the church wants to grow, the more the church will empower creative ideas, and the more stress will occur.

Some churches have been coasting (i.e., existing without any expectations for personal growth, leadership accountability, mission sensitivity, or lifestyle adjustment) for so long that they are about to go bankrupt. High stress will be the price of change.

Other churches are more balanced and healthy (i.e., they have at least some expectations for personal growth, leadership accountability, mission sensitivity, and lifestyle adjustment). Moderate stress will be the price of change.

Strategic thinkers help the congregation develop a habit or routine for personal growth, leadership accountability, mission sensitivity, and lifestyle adjustment, and radical change and creativity can be achieved with minimal stress.

Let's revisit our example of St. Anonymous Church:

The first innovation was a healing worship service, this is an innovative new idea for this mainstream, established church. Strategic thinkers understand that it aligns with vision and can be implemented within the boundaries of core values and bedrock beliefs. There are leaders to make a team. There are anticipated measurable results. Therefore, the healing service is on the working list for strategic thinkers.

Strategic thinkers have been briefed by the mission team. They understand, and occasionally have reality tested, the teams' answers to the questions *when*, *how*, and *where*. They begin to understand "how much" it will really cost.

- There will be stress over tradition and attitude. Not only is the denomination not well known for offering healing worship choices, but the local tradition in this well-educated, affluent community is suspicious of miracles and reliant on modern medical science. Cures for cancer have a lot more to do with proper chemotherapy than with profound faith. There will be some serious education and personal growth that will need to happen. Members will need to revisit their denominational history, reconsider their assumptions about God's miraculous intervention, and probably broaden their understanding of prayer.

- There will be some stress over leadership and organization. The healing worship team members will need to travel beyond their region to observe examples of healing worship and receive mentoring from other leaders—and there is no seminary continuing education course on the subject that they know about. Moreover, the church has a worship committee that will need to let go of some of their traditional oversight and trust the worship team to be innovative.

- There will be considerable stress over property and technology. In order to reach the target public, the healing worship service will be held in rented multipurpose space proximate to the medical centers in the city. Worship aids (kneeling rails, altars, vessels for holy oil and water) will need to be portable and symbols crucial to faith (crosses, images, words to liturgy and song) will have to be virtually projected by computer. These will be beyond the common experience of many elderly members.

- There will be minimal financial stress. The partnership with another nonprofit organization means that rental costs will be small. Equipment can be acquired through limited seed money by the church and the personal giving of enthusiastic team members.

In short, the real cost of discipleship for the healing worship service will involve personal growth among members, different lines of accountability in the organization, and sensitivity to the mission field. Team members are already adjusting their lifestyles to accomplish the mission.

The second goal of St. Anonymous involved the Bible study program. The small Bible study group has been an ongoing program for several years. It clearly aligns with the "DNA" of the church (values, beliefs, vision, and mission). It has committed leaders. However, for the past two years it has not been able to deliver anticipated results. New members have not joined; the group has not multiplied; and spiritual enthusiasm has waned. As strategic thinkers dialogue with the mission team, it becomes clear that certain key tactics must change. The time and place (*when* and *where*) are fine, but how the small Bible study group works will change:

- The leaders of the small group must refocus energy away from actually leading the group to mentoring emerging leaders and allowing them to experiment and grow by leading the group.

- The learning methodology of the small group must shift from print to video in order to attract younger participants. This will include video clips from selected movies and television programs, and video segments of scholars personally interpreting scriptures.

Now that strategic thinkers understand these significant changes, they can measure the true "cost" of the program. The key cost centers will be the following:

- Attitude change: Older Bible study participants will need to change their perceptions of young adults to recognize them as equally mature but in a different way.

- Leadership change: The current Bible study leaders will need to refocus their attention toward mentoring emerging leaders rather than actually teaching lessons.

- Technology change: The current participants will need to understand the importance of visual learning and gain computer and projection skills.

The actual financial cost will be minimal to acquire equipment and subscribe to several Internet websites to download video clips.

Imagine that a prayer chain is a ministry of the church that has been going on for decades and is considered essential ("sacred") by the church. Although it is clearly aligned with the mission and identity of the church, last year the prayer chain was not implemented because no one felt called to be a leader. That year of inactivity was painful, but congregational prayer leaders have emerged for the new program year and developed a plan for the prayer chain.

The third goal of St. Anonymous involved the prayer strategy. There are two tactical keys for the revitalized prayer chain. The first tactic changes when and where the prayer chain gathers. In fact, in the recent past the prayer chain participants never gathered at any time. Now the leaders will initiate a regular face-to-face gathering of the group early Saturday morning over breakfast at the church. Prayer chain participants will be required to meet regularly (without missing more than one breakfast each month). The second tactic changes how the prayer chain communicates. In addition to telephone calls, they will use an exclusive, simply designed Internet program like Facebook.

Strategic thinkers now know what the major costs of discipleship will be.

- Organization change: This is a huge step up in accountability for the members of the prayer chain. They are now being asked to take prayer so seriously that they will be required to gather as a small group for mutual encouragement, Bible conversation, and growing intimacy.

  Strategic thinkers can anticipate significant stress over this step in accountability. The idea that anyone might be dropped from the prayer chain because of inactivity or inability to attend small group meetings contradicts their sense of privilege. Being a "prayerful person" and being a "prayer warrior" are two different things.

- Property change: Saturday morning breakfasts in this small church will require modifications to the kitchen and basement. Not only will the prayer team need access to the facilities but tables will need to be set up in advance. The refrigerator will need to be repaired and perhaps a microwave purchased.

  Strategic thinkers can anticipate stress over expectations for breakfast. Younger participants won't appreciate the fried food and weak tea that is a staple diet for the older generation; and the older generation will need to learn to appreciate and respect the tastes of younger people for fine coffee and fresh fruit.

- Technology change: The plan assumes that prayer chain participants will acquire hardware and software in order to keep up with everyone on the team, all at once, continuously through the day.

169

Strategic thinkers know that Internet communication is going to be a huge learning curve for a number of traditional participants in the prayer chain. They will also find it difficult to adapt to the habit of text messaging prayers by the younger participants. They will struggle to realize that these new technologies are not just "new-fangled ways" of doing things but tactic adapted to the fast-paced world around them.

The financial cost is modest since participants will donate money to provide breakfast, and every household already has a computer with family members online. Members of the youth have already volunteered to coach senior members of the prayer chain in how to use the Internet chat forum.

The fourth goal of St. Anonymous involved the outreach ministry. The Food Bank is a successful ministry now at a turning point in its life. It began as the creative idea of two leaders only a year ago, and has rapidly expanded in both donors and clients. Not only does it align with the mission of the church but the volunteers are exemplary in modeling core values. They considered becoming a nonprofit corporation, but decided against it, fearing that government grants might limit their ability to share faith.

Their proposal to the leadership summit indicates two new tactics. Both of them are going to be expensive, but the team is convinced that people will contribute money if they truly understand and celebrate the scope of the mission.

- Leadership change: The food bank is now large enough that volunteers alone are not sufficient. The team needs to hire a part-time operations officer and expand the position to full-time within two years. Their decision to remain a clearly faith-based ministry of the church reduces some of their grant application options and makes them more dependent on giving from the church and wider community. They will need to raise significantly more dollars each year.

- Property change: The second challenge is that they have run out of space. They were operating from a basement room of the church, but the space has become too small for storage and display. Moreover, the current space isn't easily accessible to the elderly, physically disabled, or mothers with small children. And the truth is that the damp, musty basement space blocks them from expanding to fresh foods and baked goods. The final consideration is that their community research reveals that a significant number of needy people are so angry at the church that they refuse to come to the church building even when they are hungry. Altogether there is a compelling need to relocate to rented space.

This is a strong, healthy church that has made a practice of sound planning for many years. Therefore, the strategic thinkers in the leadership summit anticipate minimal stress for personal growth, leadership accountability, and mission sensitivity. However, the church is itself relatively poor, so the financial stress will be considerable.

All these changes involve money (especially the new strategy for the Food Bank), and St. Anonymous considers itself as a "poor church." The stewardship leaders addressed the financial concern using the ComparativeInsite Report. They were able to objectively define the true financial potential of the congregation.

The leaders reviewed the original search area that defined the current "reach" of the congregation. This included 252 households, or 97.2 percent of the church. MissionInsite provided the median incomes for every lifestyle segment represented in the church starting from the largest to the smallest.

Code	Top Lifestyle Segments in the Congregation	% of Con-gregation	# of Member Households	Median Income by Segment	Est. Cong HH Median Income
L42	Rooted Flower Power	13.9%	35	$54,827	$1,918,929
C11	Aging of Aquarius	11.5%	29	$119,041	$3,452,180
J34	Aging in Place	10.3%	26	$62,121	$1,615,139
E20	No Place like Home	7.5%	19	$72,696	$1,381,233
K40	Bohemian Groove	4.4%	11	$36,435	$400,790

O53	Colleges and Cafés	4.0%	10	$32,796	$327,964
E21	Unspoiled Splendor	3.6%	9	$72,801	$410,619
O51	Digital Dependents	3.6%	9	$45,624	$410,619
Q64	Town Elders	3.6%	9	$26,236	$236,122
Q62	Reaping Rewards	3.2%	8	$40,886	$327,085
B09	Family Fun-tastic	2.5%	7	$98,008	$686,058
R66	Dare to Dream	2.8%	7	$27,202	$190,415
M45	Diapers and Debit Cards	2.4%	6	$44,939	$269,633
D18	Suburban Attainment	2.4%	6	$71,900	$431,401
J36	Settled and Sensible	2.4%	6	$45,159	$270,952
P56	Midscale Medley	2.0%	5	$45,511	$227,556
E 19	Full Pockets Empty Nests	2.0%	5	$72,731	$363,653
I31	Blue Collar Comfort	1.6%	4	$66,249	$264,997
D15	Sports Utility Families	1.6%	4	$94,307	$377,229
G24	Status Seeking Singles	1.6%	4	$67,996	$271,985
I30	Stockcars and State Parks	1.2%	3	$69,978	$209,934
C14	Boomers and Boomerangs	1.2%	3	$92,873	$278,618
A04	Picture Per-fect Families	1.2%	3	$180,101	$540,302
C13	Silver Sophisticates	1.2%	3	$98,065	$294,194
S69	Urban Survivors	1.2%	3	$26,505	$79,516
O54	Striving Single Scene	0.8%	2	$32,415	$64,830

O55	Family Troopers	0.8%	2	$36,397	$72,793
Q65	Senior Discounts	0.8%	2	$17,512	$35,024
F23	Families Matter Most	0.8%	2	$68,703	$137,406
R67	Hope for Tomorrow	0.8%	2	$18,140	$36,281
K37	Wired for Success	0.8%	2	$49,943	$99,886
S71	Tough Times	0.4%	1	$13,115	$13,115
F 22	Fast Track Couples	0.4%	1	$74,789	$74,789
A02	Platinum Prosperity	0.4%	1	$317,568	$317,568
Total Estimated Gross Income					$16,434,633
Estimated Total Net (Less 25% Tax Bracket)					$12,325,975

Although the tax brackets among church members differed, the stewardship leaders chose to be cautious and based calculation on a 25 percent income bracket. This was the result:

Based on Gross Income			Based on Net Income (Example: 25% Tax bracket)	
2% of Income	334,692		2% of Income	246,519
3% of income	493,038		3% of income	369,779
5% of Income	821,731		5% of Income	616,298
7% of Income	1,150,424		7% of Income	862,818
10% of Income	1,643,463		10% of Income	1,232,597

The previous year's budget was $300,000, but the church ended the year with a $10,000 deficit. Average giving could objectively be estimated a little higher than 2 percent. The calculation revealed that if average giving increased to just 3 percent, the church could reasonably add almost $70,000 to the next year's budget. Many members of St. Anonymous were shocked by the result. They had always perceived themselves as a "poor church," and suddenly they realized they were richer than they thought!

"How much will it cost?" Strategic thinkers automatically measure the cost in order of priority. If there is a financial cost, the thought process helps you detail exactly what needs financial support. Even if there is no financial cost, the thought process helps you measure stress and plan ahead for intervention.

Chapter 7

The Sustainability of Strategic Thinking

It would seem logical that the *way of strategic thinking* would automatically lead to the *sustainability of strategic thinking*. And if church leaders get in the habit of annual research, spiritual discernment, and assessment, this connection does happen. Unfortunately, the habit of strategic thinking too often breaks down.

The reason it breaks down is that churches today confuse strategic thinking with institutional survival. In a sense, that is an easy mistake to make. After all, strategic planning focuses on program development. This leads to anxiety about finances. And institutional survival is necessary in order to provide financial resources. Strategic planning usually bogs down when churches believe they can't afford current programs or innovative ideas.

The body of Christ is addicted to church institutions. The addiction began in the fourth century with the emergence of Christendom, and it continues today among established churches of all traditions and denominations. We aren't conscious of it, but we continually return to it. Just as a drug addict can't even conceive of daily living without the combination of personal obligations, financial expectations, and the drug "fix" that will buy time to meet obligations; so also today's church can't even conceive of a Christian year without the combination of sacred programs, financial needs, and the institution that will buy time to perpetuate the programs.

Originally, the body of Christ was never addicted to institutions. But it was dependent on leadership succession! There was an organizational theory behind their strategic thinking, but it had nothing to do with buildings, repetitive programs, salaries, or denominational polities. Yes, these *might* be useful tactics for future leaders to use to pursue God's mission; but they were not *essential* to the mission. The only essential was the ability to hand off responsibility and authority to emerging leaders who would carry on the good work. In the fourth century, apostolic succession became confused with institutional survival, and the mistake has continued to this day.

Although I have described program development, property and technology development, and financial potential as options for the pursuit of God's mission, the emphasis of strategic thinking is always on leadership development. The priorities and measureable outcomes that emerge from strategic thinking aren't delegated to the committees of an institution but to leaders and teams who are free to act and innovate in any way that will get the desired and faithful results. They *might* need property and technology, but then again they *might not*. They *might* need paid personnel, but then again they *might not*. They *might* need to initiate a capital campaign, but then again they *might not*. The key to success for strategic *planning* is the institution, but the key to success for strategic *thinking* is a leadership team.

This contrast is most visible when we examine the two different functions of an annual congregational meeting.

The addictive habit of the church is to position the annual meeting as another layer of strategic *planning*. The results of research, discernment, and assessment that culminate in a leadership summit are then *referred to the annual meeting*. (In some traditions, the referral is to an ecclesiastical hierarchy in which other denominational officials must approve or disapprove the priorities of leadership.) Research, discernment, and assessment are revisited all over again. The priorities of leadership are adjusted to fit the finances of the institution. And since the lion's share of institutional budgets goes to overhead costs, very little is allocated to programs. This dramatically limits the innovation of leaders and almost guarantees the perpetuation of the same programs whether they are effective or not. Governments encourage the addiction to institutionalism because they usually insist that they elect trustees, approve budgets, and generally report to the relevant government tax authority.

If there is an annual congregational meeting, it will function much differently in the way of strategic *thinking*. Here, the only point of an annual meeting is to regularly define, refine, and celebrate core values, bedrock beliefs, motivating vision, and mission of the church. It focuses on Heart Beat, Heart Song, and *heartburst*. There is no micromanagement. They never second guess the decisions of their spiritual leaders. Annual meetings aren't really about planning. They are about faithfulness. They demonstrate the passion and calling of the people to follow the vision God has set before them.

The church trusts the pastor and board. The pastor and board trust the teams. This is not blind trust. The reason that delegation is included in this section on perspiration is that spiritual leaders must have *reasonable* trust for each other and for the teams that will implement strategies.

Blind trust occurs when churches live in a fog about core values and beliefs, vision and mission; and when ends policies, decision-making habits, and executive limitations are vague and merely assumed instead of clear and intentionally instilled. *Blind* trust occurs when churches don't follow a rigorous, consistent, and universal process to hire (or acquire) leaders, train leaders, evaluate leaders, and (if necessary) fire staff or dismiss volunteer leaders. *Blind* trust always results in limited delegation and constant supervision. Leaders are given responsibility but not authority to act. This means teams must first submit plans and wait for approvals before implementation. This slows down decision making, and over time the church loses momentum for mission and relevancy to the mission field.

Reasonable trust occurs when churches are clear about values, beliefs, vision, and mission; measureable outcomes are clearly defined; and decision-making habits and executive limitations provide boundaries within which teams can do whatever they deem effective to achieve the outcomes expected but beyond which they cannot go. Leaders are given both responsibility and authority to act. This speeds up decision making, and over time the church sustains momentum and relevancy.

In recent years, there has been a rebellious movement against the addiction to institutions. Logically, this has implied a refusal to do strategic *planning*. Innovated and anti-institutional movements have encouraged entrepreneurs to work outside the institution to create creative ministries without the overhead of ecclesiastical buildings, salaries, and polities. There are two problems:

- Such ministries are rarely sustainable. They come; they go. While this is often celebrated by those who do the ministry, it may well be irresponsible to the people who receive the ministry. The ministry raises the hopes of a particular public only to abandon them, their families, and their networks later on.

- Ironically, these same innovators (who value freedom from the institutional church) are later organizing to get seed money from the institutional church. In theory they are independent, but in practice they are utterly dependent on the very institutions they criticize.

One is reminded of Jesus's parable of the seeds falling on rocky soil that spring up quickly but fade in the heat of the day. The soil is too shallow. Their roots aren't deep enough. When ministry eschews strategic *planning* without practicing strategic *thinking*, what was initially effective rapidly becomes ineffective.

The key question for innovative ministries (including church plants, alternative faith communities, etc.) is this: Do you have a plan to hand off leadership to the next generation? This is not about institutions. It is about leadership. Whether they are paid or unpaid, ordained or lay, and housed or peripatetic is irrelevant. But leadership succession is crucial. That is the way of strategic thinking.

Strategic thinking that follows a process of research, discernment, and assessment culminates in delegating responsibility and authority to a leader or team. Note that an effective leadership succession plan delegates *both* responsibility *and* authority. The Christendom process of strategic planning only delegated responsibility, but authority was held by the congregational meeting or institutional bureaucracy. That's why they micromanage the strategic plan. But strategic *thinking* delegates both responsibility and authority. The role of the annual meeting or bureaucracy is to define, refine, and celebrate the foundation of trust and the power of vision—and in some traditions they might commission leaders and bless them on their innovative way.

There is a standard template for delegating responsibility and authority to trusted teams. The template parallels job descriptions for staff and mandates for teams.

- Restate the foundation of trust, vision, and mission of the church as a whole.

- Define the rationale or purpose of the ministry.

- Identify the public(s) that the strategy is intended to bless.

- Identify the name of the leader or team.

- Identify any partners within or beyond the church for future collaboration.

- Define the measureable outcomes that should result in *acceleration* and/or *impact*.

- Identify any particular executive limitations that must guide *when*, *where*, or *how* the strategy must be developed.

- Identify any particular cost centers that will need to be addressed.

- Anticipate any particular stress that might occur.

- Indicate the time for evaluation and possible termination of the strategy.

Note that the template to delegate responsibility and authority doesn't include any specific list of tasks to be performed or tactics to be used. Delegation is ultimately pragmatic. Teams do whatever works, functioning within boundaries, to achieve desired results.

Strategic thinking eventually demands delegation of authority and responsibility. But the same connection happens in reverse. The exercise of both authority and responsibility demands strategic thinking. The leadership summit empowers true teams, and true teams inform a leadership summit. This dynamic is usually mirrored by organizational structure.

The work of the board and senior staff focuses on sustaining identity and aligning vision, community research and spiritual discernment, policy development and prioritization, and long-term planning. The work of the teams and program staff focuses on growing leaders and maturing teams, implementation and problem solving, church assessment and effectiveness, and short-term planning.

This means that the leadership summit includes the board and senior staff. The summit resists the temptation to micromanage. Instead, it concentrates on considering creative ideas, rehabilitating important programs that are failing to achieve results, and terminating ineffective programs that are holding the church back. The teams resist the temptation to change outcomes or policies. They concentrate on sustaining effective programs, solving problems, and implementing new ideas.

This dynamic becomes the habitual behavior pattern for the church. The entire church *thinks strategically*. The church reacts quickly to unexpected emergencies or opportunities. The church can also be proactive to anticipate crises and act on creative ideas. The church has confidence that the board and senior staff are doing what they should be doing and that the teams and program staff are doing what *they* should be doing.

There are both short- and long-term benefits to strategic thinking. In the short term, strategies can be implemented quickly in a fast-changing world. In the long term, acceleration and impact can be sustained as ministries are evaluated and strategic adjustments are made.

New ideas multiply. Every year there will always be some new initiative and some creative action.

Ongoing programs are perfected. Every year ministry tactics are analyzed, continuing education agendas are clarified, redevelopment is focused, and ministries become more effective.

Ineffective programs are terminated. Every year some ministries end. Programs that were once effective but have ceased to be effective will no longer burden the resources of the church.

Over time, the benefits increase. The very routine of planning (for the church as a whole and/or for each ministry area) trains emerging leaders and sustains the church through changing pastoral relationships.

- Disciple making is clearly coordinated. Program silos are avoided. Leaders understand how their ministry areas link to other ministry areas and how they each contribute to a single goal.

- Programs are obviously aligned. Sidetracks are avoided. It is readily apparent both to seekers and members how each creative idea and ongoing program, budget line, or capital pool is aligned to deliver the vision of the church—*and nothing else.*

- Resources are always cherished. Burnouts are avoided. Volunteers are able to focus on their passions and callings, and no longer have doubts about wasted energy. Anticipated results allow them to plan for education and training.

Over the years, congregations that regularly use the template for planning as a church and among ministry areas will have a deeper sense of integrity and purpose. Churches are no longer niche institutions that feel powerless to change the world; nor are they conglomerates of seemingly arbitrary community programs. They steadily, persistently, and purposefully advance God's mission to bless the world.

Chapter 8

The Essence of Strategic Thinking

The essence of strategic thinking is to shoot an arrow straight into the heart of the community. It is about simultaneous church growth *and* community development. That arrow is a straight line from the Heart Beat of the faith community—toward the *heartburst* of the surrounding community, guided by the Heart Song of God's unique love for specific publics. God's movement accelerates and the community is blessed. Strategic thinking sheds the deadweight of unproductive programs, avoids the sidetracks of internally or externally imposed agendas, and overcome the roadblocks of cost and stress.

Strategic Thinking

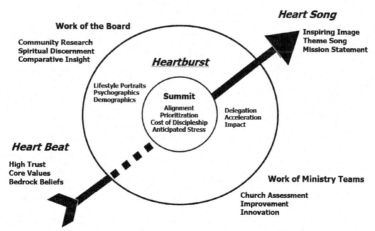

The Heart Beat of the church is the consistent, universal, and accountable trust among church members and leaders; and the faithful, predictable, and disciplined trust between church participants and God. The heartburst of the church is the urgent desire to bless particular publics or lifestyle segments in the diverse community in the spirit of Christ. The Heart Song of the church is the experience of God, awareness of God's calling, and love for God's people that motivates and guides every leader, member, and ministry of the church.

There is a method to strategic thinking, and today it is informed by sophisticated demographic and lifestyle research like that from www .MissionInsite.com. This helps the board and senior staff to research the everchanging community, and discern their spiritual yearnings and physical needs. They constantly compare lifestyle representation of church and community to go reach further and go deeper in mission. This also helps ministry teams and program staff to assess the effectiveness of church activities. They test the relevancy and success of ministries measured by outcomes.

There is a convergence of insight and urgency in strategic thinking. Board, staff, and ministry teams come together to perfectly align ongoing ministries to vision and define future goals for the acceleration of mission and positive impact in the world. They fix flagging ministries, terminate ineffective programs, and prioritize new ideas. They measure the true cost of discipleship, and anticipate the stress of constant change.

Finally, strategic thinking is sustainable with less oversight, fewer meetings, minimal conflict, and consistent empowerment. Ministry is focused and delegated to trusted teams with full responsibility and authority to do whatever it takes to achieve the anticipated outcomes defined by the church. The focus of strategic thinking is on leadership and people, rather than programs and finances. So long as teams are guided by the vision, stay within boundaries, and achieve results, they do not need a board to revisit their activities. They only bring to the summit problems they cannot seem to resolve themselves, recommendation to terminate irrelevant ministries, and big ideas to grow the church and bless the community.

Strategic thinking connects organizational identity and vision with creative integrity and positive outcomes. It begins with trust and ends with delegation. Along the way, it strives to understand the public, discern God's will for the future of both church and community, and evaluate progress so far. The dynamic of prioritization and perspiration on one hand, and implementation and problem solving on the other hand, empowers the church to be reactive and proactive at the same time.

You have often heard church leaders complain about what they call the "Tyranny of the Urgent." They say that they are unable to find the time or energy to grow leaders, set priorities, consider new ideas, measure outcomes, or pray for renewed vision—because they are too busy visiting people, attending meetings, sustaining current programs, managing conflict, and running the institution. This is not the tyranny of the urgent but the tyranny of the trivial. Strategic thinking is the art of discerning the difference between the really urgent and the truly trivial, and the courage to do the first and delegate the second.

When leaders are driven by urgency rather than by triviality, the church grows and the community is loved. When leaders are driven by triviality rather than urgency, the church declines and the community is ignored. This means that many churches understand "faithfulness" backward. They often assume that God will deal with the urgency of the world, and their job is to deal with the triviality of the institution as the only agency of mission. But faithfulness is much harder than that. God expects us to deal with the urgency of the world. This means hard choices and shared trust.

Even as you read this book, you were probably tempted to get lost in the details. Many churches are unclear about trust and vision; they have never practiced community research, gone deep into spiritual discernment, or had the courage for honest evaluation. They don't know how to determine priorities and are frightened to define outcomes; and they aren't confident that their committees (or teams) won't do something really stupid or expensive. So learning how to "think strategically" is initially very hard. It is tempting to fall back into old habits and micromanage everything.

Once you learn how to think strategically, however, the dynamic gets easier with every passing year. This is really about habits. Strategic thinking is a habit, just like strategic planning is a habit. They both require work, but different kinds of work.

The essence of strategic planning is to build and sustain the institutional church. But the essence of strategic thinking is to build and expand the realm of God. The former concentrates on programs, property, money, and staffing. The latter concentrates on leaders, priorities, the true cost of discipleship, and teaming. The chart below lists the top ten questions, and different discussions, of strategic planning versus strategic thinking.

Strategic Planning: Building the Institutional Church	Strategic Thinking: Building the Realm of God
Who is in charge?	How wide and deep is our trust?
What is the best compromise?	Are we passionate about our vision?
What do the members want?	What does God want??
What do the members need?	What does the community need?
What's the plan?	What are the priorities?
What tasks should we do?	What are the boundaries for our creativity?
What is the process for reporting and permission?	What are the outcomes for which we are accountable?
Will we preserve harmony?	Will we accelerate holistic growth?
Will we attract new people?	Will we change the world?
Will we survive?	Will we succeed?

Try to imagine the difference between the conversations in a leadership *retreat* and the conversations in a leadership *summit*.

The leadership *retreat* is usually held either within the church building or outside the community context in a camp or nature center. The retreat is both relaxed and urgent. It is relaxed because most of the participants have known each other for some time and represent church insiders. Participants are confident about their particular area of expertise (i.e., program silo, property, finance, marketing). The urgency of the retreat is driven by institutional survival. Whatever the plan might be, it needs to preserve harmony, balance the budget and reduce debt, honor tradition, maintain the building, and increase worship attendance. Strategic planning is really about sustaining critical mass. If they can sustain critical mass, then there should be some money and energy left over for creativity and outreach.

The chart above identifies the top ten questions that drive the conversation on retreat. Sometimes one question is more pressing than others. In any given year the church might be adjusting to a new pastor; rocked by a denominational controversy; torn by factional expectations; suffering from volunteer burnout; reeling from committee misbehavior that has caused unexpected litigation, community outrage, or financial deficits; or worried about the aging membership or contradictory demographic trends between church and community.

The strategic plan that emerges is really a long list of tasks. Responsibility to accomplish tasks is divided among existing program silos or assigned to specific paid staff. However, authority to accomplish tasks is limited. Committees will need to ask permission, especially if their ideas clash with traditional practices. And it is a *plan*. It is a step-by-step outline, blueprint, or scheme that defines the tasks to be implemented, the order of implementation, the resources allocated for implementation—and the warning that all tasks should be performed with diplomacy and minimum stress.

Of course, the community is changing fast and becoming more diverse, even as the church is struggling for stability and becoming more homogeneous. The *plan* becomes obsolete in short order, overwhelmed by circumstance. Eventually the experts declare that strategic *planning* doesn't work anymore. The leadership retreat remains relaxed but loses urgency. Those that gather provide moral support for each other and find respite from the pressures of office, but more and more busy leaders don't bother to attend.

If a church member asks a leader who was on retreat what the plan is for the future, the leader will both hand them a long list of tasks and explain all the compromises that lie behind the list, or just shrug their shoulders and promise to get through the next year.

Compare this to a leadership *summit*. The *summit* is usually held outside the church building but within the community context. The summit is also both relaxed and urgent, but for different reasons. It is relaxed because each participant reasonably trusts the other participants to model and articulate the shared core values and bedrock beliefs of the organization—even though the summit includes church members from the margins of society. The summit is urgent because everyone is passionate about the vision and mission of the church, and is eager to make a difference in the community.

Strategic *thinking* is really about critical momentum, not critical mass. Whatever the priorities and however the outcomes are defined, participants in a leadership summit believe that if they can accelerate church life and impact community change, then the costs of discipleship will be overcome. Strategic thinkers believe that if they can sustain mission momentum, then there will be money and energy left to sustain the institution.

The chart above identifies the top ten questions that drive the conversation of the summit. Sometimes one question is more pressing than others. In any given year the church might need to embed trust, revise vision, or open itself to something new from God. The community context has changed, priorities need to be readjusted, and boundaries for creativity need to be updated. Even the measurable outcomes might change to be more relevant to success. Perhaps the balance between acceleration and impact needs to be reconsidered. But above all, the leadership summit asks and answers the question, "Were we successful this year?"

The result of the leadership summit is not a long list of tasks. It is a set of priorities and clear measureable outcomes for every ministry team. Underperforming or ineffective programs will be scrutinized. Problems that couldn't be resolved by teams will be solved. Hard decisions to terminate ineffective programs (no matter how "sacred") will be made. The true cost of change will be identified. Stress will be expected and even welcomed rather than avoided. Clear delegation of responsibility *and* authority for implementation will be handed off to teams.

Of course, the community is changing just as fast or faster and becoming ever more diverse. But the church is keeping pace and becoming ever more heterogeneous. There is no "plan" to be overcome by circumstance, but there is a set of priorities and anticipated outcomes that has been delegated to trusted teams. Strategic planning might not work anymore, but leaders still make every effort to participate in the leadership summit.

If a member asks a leader who was at the leadership summit what the plan is, the leader will probably say, "I don't know. Ask the team." But the leader will be able to identify the priorities, outcomes, costs, and anticipated stress for the new year—and assure the member that, however creative the teams need to be, the integrity of the church will never be compromised and the vision of the church will always be pursued.

Once leaders make strategic thinking a habit, they will find that it gets easier every year. What may seem complicated now will soon become second nature. Leaders and members will automatically apply the methods for research and listening, assessment, prioritization, and anticipated challenges to whatever they are doing. There are many things that are remarkable about the way of strategic thinking.

The way of strategic thinking is remarkably humble. It is humble before the public: listening first and speaking last; observing before acting; empathic rather than authoritarian. It doesn't presume to know best what people need, nor does it assume that people need what their church already has.

Strategic thinking is humble before the Spirit: praying first and acting later; slaying rather than preserving sacred cows; preparing for a heartburst rather than producing a brainstorm. It doesn't presume that current member comfort zones are also the will of God.

Strategic thinking reduces management. It is based on high trust, delegating responsibility and authority for action to teams, while the senior staff and board concentrate on long-range planning. It avoids micromanagement and focuses on results rather than processes.

Yet perhaps the most remarkable thing about strategic thinking is that it changes the character of the church. The church is no longer an institution on its own but only one player in the Christian movement. Strategic thinking isn't really about producing better programs, deploying better personnel, maintaining sacred space, raising more money, or even solving social problems. It's really about sustaining a movement that generates more leaders who generate more leaders, or in more spiritual terminology, a succession of servants who mentor more servants. It's not what you do but how you think.

CPSIA information can be obtained
at www.ICGtesting.com
Printed in the USA
LVOW13s0155300617
539860LV00003B/4/P